"This book will help you stop undermini[ng]
self-criticism and start giving yourself th[e]
ment, and support you'd give to a good [...]
explanations of concepts and dozens of easy and practical exercises to
build self-confidence through self-compassion, this book has the power
to change your life."

—Kristin Neff, PhD, author of *Self-Compassion* and
associate professor, University of Texas at Austin

"Compassionate Mind approaches are one of the most exciting developments in cognitive behavior therapy. Mary Welford has written an
easy-to-read interactive book that distils the core features of developing
a different relationship with one's mind and paradoxically building one's
self-confidence."

—Professor David Veale, Institute of Psychiatry,
King's College London

"Hugely approachable, sympathetic, and fun. I'd recommend this book
to anyone wanting to improve their self-confidence. Choc-full of brilliant clinical metaphors and creative techniques, it will also be invaluable to any therapist wanting a primer on this fascinating area."

—Sam Cartwright-Hatton, clinical psychologist and
NIHR fellow, University of Sussex

"This is a wonderful book! Welford has beautifully written a remark-
able book that takes us to the heart of building self-confidence through
developing self-compassion. This book is based on a robust science of
mind that leads directly to sensitive and kind-hearted understanding
of how we develop self-critical ways of coping with difficult and stressful life experiences. This book enables you to develop an empathic
understanding of the origins of shame and also provides practical skills
and techniques in developing a compassionate mind as the basis for
self-confidence. This book is a highly accessible and practically useful
means of developing and overcoming obstacles to self-compassion."

—Professor Andrew Gumley, University of Glasgow,
UK

"Mary Welford's book is helpful, informative, and interesting. The book makes you feel very much 'looked after' and the inclusion of personal stories, including her own, gives the reader a sense of not being on their own. The approach is hugely relevant to those wishing to find their compassionate self and build their self-confidence."

—Erica Wakeman, reader

THE POWER OF SELF-COMPASSION

using compassion-focused therapy to end self-criticism and build self-confidence

MARY WELFORD, DCLINPSY

New Harbinger Publications, Inc.

Publisher's Note

This publication is designed to provide accurate and authoritative information in regard to the subject matter covered. It is sold with the understanding that the publisher is not engaged in rendering psychological, financial, legal, or other professional services. If expert assistance or counseling is needed, the services of a competent professional should be sought.

Distributed in Canada by Raincoast Books

Copyright © 2013 by Mary Welford
New Harbinger Publications, Inc.
5674 Shattuck Avenue
Oakland, CA 94609
www.newharbinger.com

First published in the UK by Constable. An imprint of Constable & Robinson Ltd.

Cover design by Amy Shoup
Acquired by Tesilya Hanauer
Edited by Brady Kahn

Library of Congress Cataloging in Publication Data

Welford, Mary.
  The power of self-compassion : using compassion-focused therapy to end self-criticism and build self-confidence / Mary Welford, DClinPsy.
       pages cm. -- (The New Harbinger compassion-focused therapy series)
  Includes bibliographical references.
  ISBN 978-1-57224-983-7 (pbk. : alk. paper) 1. Self-esteem. 2. Compassion--Psychological aspects. 3. Self-confidence. 4. Emotion-focused therapy. I. Title.
  BF697.5.S46W435 2013
  158.1--dc23
                                    2012034631

Printed in the United States of America

15   14   13

10   9   8   7   6   5   4   3   2   1   First printing

Contents

Foreword

It's long been understood that compassion is very important. The way we feel about ourselves and the way we think other people feel about us has a huge impact on our well-being. If we value and support ourselves, we are more likely to successfully negotiate all that life throws at us. This is in contrast to being self-critical and feeling that there's something wrong with us. However, it is not just common sense that tells us about the value of compassion. Recent advances in scientific studies have greatly advanced our understanding of how compassion, both from ourselves and from others, can help us to treat ourselves in ways that are respectful and improve our sense of well-being.

We live in a world where we are constantly advised to judge, rate, and evaluate ourselves. All around us are messages that we might not be good enough. Maybe our parents told us such things, or maybe at school we were often the last to be picked for the team. Of course, nowadays schools are constantly focused on tests, judgments, and evaluations of all kinds. Over the last ten to twenty years, even competitions on television have become increasingly focused on which contestant will be thrown off the show. From *Big Brother* to cookery competitions, we see people anxiously waiting to find out if they will be the one voted off, the camera following those recently ejected in their tearful departures. This may well be good for television, but it doesn't do a lot for our psychological well-being. It fosters the old view that only success and achieving and doing things can make us happy, and if we are not up to scratch or if we do something wrong, then we too will feel anxious, unhappy, and tearful. So it doesn't take much to recognize that our sense of belonging and community can be a lot more fragile than it used to be. Indeed, our focus on self-esteem and achievement, at the expense of helping, sharing, and nurturing our community, has been offered as one reason depression and anxiety are on the increase in the modern world, especially among younger people.

What research tells us, however, is that if we learn to value and respect ourselves, if we treat ourselves and others with kindness even when things are going wrong, we are much more likely to be able to cope with setbacks and be happier. While striving for success is important, seeking to be compassionate to yourself and to others has been shown time and again to be associated with a sense of well-being. After all, it's easy to become critical, harsh, and rejecting when things go wrong, but the real measure of ourselves is whether we can be supportive and encouraging when life is tough.

In this important book, Dr. Mary Welford uses her wealth of experience and knowledge in working with people with a whole range of psychological difficulties. She explores why our brains are so susceptible to reacting to life's setbacks and difficulties in the way that they do and especially why we have a tendency to judge ourselves and be self-critical. Unlike other animals, you have a brain that is constantly thinking and judging. Imagine a zebra running away from a lion. Once the zebra has escaped, it will shortly settle down to feed again. However, we humans can spend many days ruminating about what would have happened if we'd gotten caught and fantasizing about the most horrible things. Zebras and chimpanzees don't worry about what they're thinking, what they look like, or what other zebras or chimpanzees might be thinking about them! Humans, on the other hand, do—and all the time! We look in the mirror and think, *Oh gosh, is that really me? How come I have put on so much weight?* Of course, we also think about our internal worlds—the fantasies, thoughts, and feelings we have within us, and we can be critical of those too. Life becomes full of *shoulds* and *shouldn'ts* or *ought* and *ought nots* or even *musts* and *must nots*. Again, no other animal thinks, judges, dislikes, fears, or tries to avoid its fantasies, feelings, and thoughts in the way that humans do. We call this self-criticism, and many people who struggle with self-confidence can be harsh and self-critical toward themselves. By slowing down, it is possible to really explore the nature of our self-criticism and realize how constant and unpleasant it can be.

Now, of course, there are times when we certainly want to be aware of our mistakes and to improve. It's not that we are never disappointed with how things turn out, but it's rather how we deal with this disappointment. Do we deal with it openly, honestly, kindly, and supportively or harshly and aggressively, which actually makes us feel much worse? Compassion, as you will see, is not about being slapdash and careless but about being generally supportive and encouraging to do our best!

Dr. Welford helps us to understand that our susceptibility to getting caught up in negative ways of feeling and thinking about ourselves can be very unhelpful. She also helps us to recognize that, because of the way our brains are designed, it's relatively easy for us to get into the habit of putting ourselves down. Indeed, this is a universal human trait and absolutely not our fault. After all, we didn't design our brains with their various capacities for emotions, thoughts, and fantasies. Nor did we design our capacities for complex thinking and ruminating. Nor did we choose our backgrounds or our genes, both of which can make us more or less susceptible to being kind and supportive or being critical of ourselves.

We all have different genes, talents, and abilities, and we come from a whole range of backgrounds. All these serve to make us slightly different from each other. So while some people are highly intelligent and win Nobel Prizes, others are less so and struggle with basic reading and writing; while some people are great conversationalists, others are shy and struggle with what to say. A key message in this book, therefore, is that we all simply find ourselves "here" and, whatever the slings and arrows of outrageous fortune, our relationship with ourselves is very important for how we cope with life. Research shows that the more compassionate we are toward ourselves, the happier we are and the more resilient we become when faced with difficulties in our lives. In addition, we are better able to reach out to others for help, and we feel more compassionate toward other people too, making us good to have as a friend.

Compassion can sometimes be viewed as being a bit "soft" or "weak," a question of just "being nice" or "letting your guard down" and "not trying hard enough." This is a major mistake because, on the contrary, compassion requires us to be courageous and sometimes to be open to our painful feelings and to learn to tolerate them, to face up to our own problematic emotions and difficulties and the disappointments we can have in ourselves. Compassion does not mean turning away from emotional difficulties or discomforts or trying to get rid of them. Compassion means noticing when we have been critical of ourselves and acted in potentially unhelpful ways and then making a deliberate choice to be compassionate, generating inner support and encouragement. So, it is not a "soft" option; rather, compassion simply means being sensitive and aware of our distress (and of the distress of others) and genuinely committing to do something about it. There is nothing soft or weak in either of those two efforts. So, in fact, compassion helps us to build courage, honesty, and commitment to learn to cope with the difficulties we face. It enables us to do things to and for ourselves that help us to flourish and take care of ourselves—not as a demand or a requirement, but to enable us to live our lives more fully and contentedly.

In this book, Dr. Welford brings her many years of experience as a clinical psychologist and psychotherapist working with people who often feel bad about themselves for one reason or another. Maybe they carry shame from the past or are just disappointed that they can't be the way they wish to be or be more in control of their emotions. Dr. Welford outlines a model of compassion that seeks to stimulate and build our self-confidence so that we can engage with things that we find difficult. She helps us learn how to develop a supportive friendship with ourselves that will help us when times are difficult.

The approach that Dr. Welford takes is called a compassionate-mind approach because when we engage compassion, it can influence our attention, thoughts, feelings, and behavior—in other words, how our minds operate as a whole. The compassionate-mind approach draws on many other well-developed approaches, including those of Eastern traditions, such as Buddhism. In addition, compassionate-mind approaches, especially those that form part of compassion-focused therapy as seen here, are rooted in a scientific understanding of how our mind works.

Undoubtedly, over the years, this understanding of compassion and how to promote it will change and improve. One thing that is clear, however, is the fact that kindness, warmth, and understanding go a long way toward helping us when we suffer. In these pages, you will find these qualities in abundance so you too can learn to be gentle, understanding, supportive, and kind but also engaging and courageous when working through difficulties.

Many people suffer silently and secretly with a whole range of problems that can be linked to a lack of self-confidence and a tendency to be self-critical. Some feel ashamed or angry with themselves; others sometimes fear not being able to cope in particular ways. Sadly, shame can stop many of us from reaching out for help, but by opening our hearts to compassion, and recognizing our common humanity and vulnerability to suffering, we can take the first steps toward dealing with these difficulties in new and more effective ways. My compassionate wishes go with you on your journey.

—Professor Paul Gilbert, PhD, FBPsS, OBE, March 2012

Introduction

The time to repair the roof is when the sun is shining.

—John F. Kennedy

In years gone by, I would have been unable to hand over the final draft of a book without experiencing crippling self-criticism. Today I can hold my self-criticism at bay and acknowledge the fact that this book is by no means perfect, but it is the best I can do at this moment in time and that's okay. The application of the compassionate-mind approach to my personal life has taught me this, for which I am truly thankful. This is just one of the reasons I sincerely recommend it to others.

Compassion-focused therapy (CFT) was developed by Professor Paul Gilbert of Derbyshire, England. It is often referred to as the compassionate-mind approach because the therapy aims to develop and enhance compassion, and particularly self-compassion, to influence an individual's attention, thoughts, feelings, and behavior—in other words, all aspects of the mind. The term *compassionate-mind approach* is used throughout this book.

Professor Gilbert has both helped and worked alongside a large number of people experiencing difficulties. He has also taught, supervised, and mentored a team of therapists and researchers who have been able to contribute to the development of the therapy. I am privileged to say I am part of this team.

The compassionate-mind approach is informed by a wide range of theories and areas of research, such as evolution, neuroscience, and psychology. It also uses a range of exercises that have been found to be helpful. Although some have been drawn from Eastern traditions, such as Buddhism, it is important to note that in this approach, such exercises have been isolated from their religious or spiritual origins and are used on a purely secular basis.

In the compassionate-mind approach, the aim is to address self-criticism and build self-confidence through the development of self-compassion. We all have different beliefs, and it is understandable that not everyone reading this will believe the same things I believe. My goal is to respect different views but also be true to how I see things. I believe in evolution. I personally believe that we have evolved from single-celled organisms, from reptiles and from apes. I believe that something termed "natural selection" had a central role in driving evolution, making certain traits, characteristics, physical attributes and skills more common and other things less so. However, I am also aware that natural selection may not be the only influencing factor in this process. It might not be the only thing that accounts for how we are today. I personally believe that other answers will come from science, but I am also aware that we may not know for sure.

Some people believe that something or someone else had a role to play in the process of evolution and has guided things. Others believe that human beings were created and are not descended from any other animal life. If these or any other beliefs make you question what is written here, please do not simply turn away.

Hopefully, we can agree that we each have a very complicated brain that has evolved at least since human beings existed (and that in itself is a very long time). In addition, our brain development is influenced by our experiences, and we will look at this in a lot more detail later. As such, the human brain is equipped with many amazing capacities, but many difficult and conflicting qualities as well, all of which we have to deal with and work out. I hope that agreeing this may assist those who don't believe in evolution to still get something out of this book.

The book starts by outlining the way in which the compassionate-mind approach views self-confidence. With a better understanding of how the human emotional systems behave and regulate each other, you will be made aware of how you may be undermining yourself. To counteract this, you will then be guided through a range of exercises aimed at building your self-confidence.

HOW TO USE THIS BOOK

If you decided to learn to swim, it wouldn't be wise to throw yourself in at the deep end. Instead, you would probably start by going to your local pool at a quiet time, getting into the shallow end, and gradually progressing to more and more difficult challenges as you built up your confidence with being in the water.

It may be helpful for you to think similarly about how you follow the exercises in this book. In other words, start gradually, when things are relatively easy for you. The term *easy* is used loosely here because, of course, life is rarely easy, but it is likely that there are some times in your day, week, month, or even year that are better suited to certain tasks than others. Choose to start when you can predict life will be less hectic and you will have the time and space to focus your efforts.

Take Your Time

One of the fundamental principles guiding the compassionate-mind approach is that intellectual understanding does not necessarily bring about emotional change. In other words, while on an intellectual level we may know that we are loved or accepted by others, on an emotional level we may not feel it. Although many of the exercises in this book aim to address this gap between thinking and feeling, potentially one of the most powerful things you can do throughout this work is to take time to reflect and allow what you have learned to sink in. In other words, think about how the information you have been given relates to you and your own situation and pause regularly to consider this for seconds, minutes, hours, or longer.

Make a record of this process too. Something as simple as writing notes and reviewing them in the future can help you further narrow the gap between knowing something and feeling it.

Practical Preparation

This book incorporates a number of worksheets, additional copies of which are freely available from the Compassionate Mind website (www.compassionatemind.co.uk). To supplement the worksheets, you may want to purchase, find, or make a journal or notebook in which you can keep ongoing notes and reflections. In addition, you can use this journal for exercises such as writing compassionate letters.

Many people find it helpful to always use a specific pen or pencil when undertaking these tasks. I personally associate ball-point pens with work, and they therefore can trigger associated thoughts or feelings. For this reason, I always use a felt-tip pen when writing in my journal. View your writing utensils as props to support you in building your self-confidence. In years to come, they will act as a reminder of how far you have arrived in the development of your self-confidence and serve as a prompt for practices that may be helpful for you to continue.

Book Structure

The book consists of two key stages. The first involves looking at the concept of self-confidence in the context of our evolution, biology, and life experiences. This will be the main focus of chapters 1, 2, and 3. The second stage involves doing exercises that help to build self-confidence by the application of self-compassion.

In the last chapter, you will be encouraged to reflect upon which parts you have found most helpful and use these to continue building your self-confidence in the future. In order to help you with this, a personal practice summary sheet, containing a list of all the exercises that may be beneficial to you, is provided at the end of the preface. Space has been left for you to make notes on how useful you find each exercise and to record any additional thoughts for future guidance. Some exercises included here may be ones you choose to do daily or weekly, while others may be exercises you do much less frequently.[1]

Finally, although self-help can be beneficial, in some circumstances it may not be enough. There is no shame in this. It's the reason friends and family members confide in each other, and why thousands of psychological therapists like myself have jobs. At such times, we can all best help ourselves by requesting or accepting help from others, be they friends, family, or professionals. If you think you require professional help, your doctor should be able to advise you about the options open to you.

---

1   A range of exercises included in this book do not appear on the summary sheet. These exercises are not to be used as personal practice but instead are meant to illustrate and illuminate particular points, to aid reflection on your journey, or to help you work through initial obstacles.

Personal Practice Summary Sheet

Exercise	Usefulness	Additional Notes
Mindfulness of sound		
Mindfulness of bodily sensations		
Mindfulness of breathing		
Mindfulness of a visual anchor point		
Mindfulness of a tactile anchor point		
Mindful walking		
Soothing-rhythm breathing		
Finding your place of contentment		

Being deeply compassionate		
Reexperiencing your own compassion		
The ideal compassionate self		
Evoking a memory of compassion from others		
Turning compassion outward		
Compassion for those who lack self-confidence		
Turning compassion inward		
Compassion for your own journey and situation		
Developing your compassionate coach		

Exercise	Usefulness	Additional Notes
Recognizing thoughts and images that have occupied your mind		
Noticing thoughts and images as they occur in your mind		
Giving your new and compassionate brain a voice		
Two chairs		
Compassionate letter writing to build your self-confidence		
Compassionate letter writing from the compassionate role to yourself		
Writing a compassionate letter based on compassionate alternative thoughts and images		
Identifying your personal goals toward building your self-confidence		
Identifying the steps you need to take		

Using compassionate imagery to prepare for social situations								
Using compassionate imagery to prepare for any situation								
Using compassionate alternative thoughts and images to prepare for taking action								
Using compassionate letter writing to access inner support								
Preparing for a compassionate behavioral experiment								
Doing your compassionate behavioral experiment								
Reviewing your compassionate behavioral experiment								
Communicating how you feel and what your needs are								
Giving constructive feedback								

Exercise	Usefulness	Additional Notes
Making seemingly small changes		
Savoring positive experiences		
Accepting yourself and things that you cannot change		
Embracing who you are		
Accepting your situation, right here, right now		
Guiding your day		
Using self-compassion in difficult situations		
Updating your formulation		
Your personal plan for the future		

1

Self-Confidence Is Something We Build and Maintain, Not Something We Have

Don't go through life, grow through life.

—Eric Butterworth

Our level of self-confidence can have a huge impact on the way things turn out for us. Take Jim, for example. He wanted to ask Becky out, but when he bumped into her, his self-confidence failed him. Instead of suggesting they go out, he ended up talking about something completely different. *What an idiot!* he told himself afterward. Whether it be taking exams, going for job interviews, sorting out conflicts, starting a new hobby, making friends, or any other form of initiative taking, the outcome can be greatly influenced by the level of self-confidence with which we approach the task. And all of us, at some point in our lives, feel we could do with a bit more of it.

So what is self-confidence? A dictionary definition might be something like "trusting in your abilities," "having faith in yourself," or "having self-assurance." Self-confidence is actually difficult to pin down because it will differ from person to person. It may be summarized as the way you feel about yourself, either in relation to things you want to do or to your own persona.

You will probably have noticed that your self-confidence varies from day to day, situation to situation. In certain arenas, you may feel very self-confident yet in other arenas feel almost exactly the opposite. Sometimes you may find that in two seemingly similar situations your self-confidence levels will vary widely. This can be both puzzling and frustrating.

But self-confidence is not restricted to the way you react in certain situations or to how you believe others will perceive you. Self-confidence in relation to your own personality, thoughts, and feelings, the things you like about yourself and the things you don't, can greatly influence the life you lead.

WHERE DOES IT ALL START?

While it is true that some babies seem naturally more sociable and robust than others, it is difficult to pinpoint exactly where this starts. Self-confidence is likely to be influenced by genetics, time in the womb, and experiences in the early days and weeks post-birth. However, for all of us, the interesting thing about self-confidence is that we build it by first not having any. Think about how you first learned to walk. It is likely that you initially struggled to your feet, fell over, cried, and then got to your feet once more. This will have happened over and over again until eventually you were running about and climbing trees.

In those early days, you simply knew what to do, and this helped build your self-confidence. Then what happened later on, as an adult? How would or did you develop the self-confidence to drive a car, for instance? After all, almost everyone who finds him- or herself behind the wheel of a car for the first time will lack self-confidence, and anxiety may be sky high.

But step-by-step, by continuing to learn despite your anxiety, self-confidence builds until eventually you become a reasonable driver. So building self-confidence is about developing ourselves by doing things despite our anxiety.

This is one of the key principles of this book: self-confidence is something we build. Even if you are starting from the point of having little or no self-confidence in a specific area or, indeed, a range of different situations, with time and effort there is great potential for change. You can build your self-confidence.

However, like many things in life, self-confidence is something we also need to work to maintain. And so this book is all about the processes by which we first build and then maintain self-confidence.

THE FIRST SECRET OF BUILDING SELF-CONFIDENCE: BEWARE OF YOUR OWN UNDERMINING

Before looking in more detail at the ways in which self-confidence is built, you need to be aware of a very important fact. One of the reasons we may lack self-confidence is because we ourselves actually undermine it; we simply don't allow it to grow and develop. Indeed, one of the key things to be explored in this book is how and why we *undermine* our own self-confidence and what we can do to prevent this from happening.

Consider the case of Jim again. On the spot, faced with Becky, he felt anxious and panicked by the situation. With images and thoughts about himself running through his mind, he imagined he looked awkward, red-faced, clammy, and stupid. He thought, *There's no point in trying, I'll only make a mess of it. Who would want to go out with me anyway? She's bound to say no.* So rather than risk this outcome, he avoided asking her out.

In contrast, now imagine that in the days or weeks before bumping into Becky, whenever Jim pondered asking her out, he had thought,

This is going to be difficult, so I'll practice what to say...talk to a friend...get some advice. If Jim had been able to do this, the outcome might have been very different.

You can probably empathize with some aspects of Jim's undermining thoughts. Notice that when able to generate inner support, he realizes and acknowledges both his anxiety and his lack of self-confidence. It is not that he is suddenly super confident and free of anxiety. Instead, he recognizes that the task is going to be difficult and, in a self-supportive way, works through how he can prepare for and approach it. This is in marked contrast to undermining his own self-confidence by telling himself rather unpleasant things.

Here's another example of self-undermining. Imagine learning to drive while constantly telling yourself *I'll never get the hang of this...I'm bound to crash...the instructor's just not telling me how bad I am because she wants her weekly fee.* This way of thinking can't help but undermine you and make you feel more anxious. Of course, it is not just our thoughts that can undermine us in such a situation; often it is how we feel about ourselves that is our undoing. If we feel stupid, inept, and incompetent, this can in turn lead to undermining thoughts, images, and debilitating anxiety.

By contrast, suppose you think, *It's perfectly normal to feel anxious, grind the gears, bump into the curb, and have cars blowing their horns at me. I am a learner, after all.* Imagine simultaneously viewing that scenario with a sense of courage, acceptance, and empathy for your own situation. If this were the case, you would be far more likely to ride the ups and downs of the learning process successfully.

THE SECOND SECRET OF BUILDING SELF-CONFIDENCE: SELF-COMPASSION

This book will talk a lot about self-compassion, so at this point it would be helpful to consider what compassion does and does not constitute.

People have a range of ideas about compassion. The simplest definition is a sensitivity to the pain (be it psychological or physical) that we or others may experience, plus a motivation and genuine commitment to relieve it. It is the latter part of this definition that is most often overlooked. People often omit the more active component of compassion while emphasizing its other elements such as kindness, emotional warmth, and gentleness. While in certain situations self-compassion may predominantly involve these elements, the compassionate-mind approach also stresses the importance of other key aspects of compassion, such as our ability to encourage, support, and even push ourselves at the appropriate times.

Self-compassion is not about sitting in a bath surrounded by candles, buying yourself some flowers, or treating yourself to something lovely to eat—not unless such things are in your best interest. Self-compassion is about recognizing when we are struggling and about making a commitment to do what we can to improve things for ourselves step-by-step. As such, it may involve making a commitment to develop a hobby, get fit, or eat a healthier diet. It may involve facing a specific situation despite feeling high levels of anxiety, or it may be letting yourself cry or feel angry about something that has happened because you need and deserve to do so. It may also be about addressing problems with drinking, drugs, or overeating, or anything else that is holding you back in life.[1]

To illustrate this, consider Helen's story. Helen had been suffering from agoraphobia and had been a prisoner in her own house for over ten years without having the self-confidence to address the problem. Developing self-compassion did not involve her saying *There there, never mind* to herself and then surfing the Net to buy lots of lovely things to compensate. Developing self-compassion in Helen's case meant warmly acknowledging that, in her own best interest, things needed to change. Self-compassion then involved her taking courageous steps to build her self-confidence until, despite feeling intense fear, she eventually opened her front door and stepped out onto the street. Self-compassion for her meant that she reassured herself when things went wrong, recognized the difficult steps she was taking, and then courageously continued toward her goal.

---

1   Kenneth Goss has written a book for the Compassionate Mind series specifically looking at ways of addressing overeating: *The Compassionate-Mind Guide to Ending Overeating.* See the resources section.

CONCLUSIONS

In this opening chapter, you have seen that self-confidence is some-thing we build, not something we are simply born with. The way we go about building our self-confidence is crucial because we all need to be able to function while living with anxiety and uncertainty. It's this process of how we keep going when things get difficult for us that is central to the compassionate-mind approach. By learning how to be compassionate to yourself, you will have a greater chance of building the self-confidence that will sustain you in times of difficulty.

And Finally...

Having read this first chapter, and at the end of each subsequent chapter, you may want to take some time to reflect on what you've learned and make a few notes in your journal or notebook. These notes may be on points you particularly wish to remember or on how you think the topics that were discussed may apply to you personally.

2

Understanding the Impact of Evolution on Us

We are born with a tricky brain that we
did not design. That is not our fault.

—Paul Gilbert

The compassionate-mind approach views all organisms on the planet as belonging to what Paul Gilbert terms "the flow of life." In other words, human beings are viewed as existing here in their current form by virtue of evolution, just as every other species on earth has evolved. If you look at the natural world around you, you will see animals competing for and fighting over status and territory, vying for food and for mates—sometimes forming bonds that will last a lifetime, sometimes having multiple partners. In addition to this, many animals, but particularly mammals, form attachments to their young and feed and protect them from danger. They form friendships with peers and live in social groups where the prosperity of one affects that of the group and vice versa. These basic patterns of life are also recognizable within human existence, and self-confidence is central to them all.

We want the self-confidence to develop and maintain friendships, attract sexual partners, be an effective parent, and be successful in our work.

OUR EMOTION REGULATION SYSTEMS

To help us navigate the array of different activities that we as human beings engage in, we have systems in our brains to make us interested in and excited about achieving important goals. We also have systems that make us wary and protect us in case things go wrong or we could get hurt. The compassionate-mind approach uses what is known about the brain to help us understand how these systems actually work, for if we can truly understand ourselves better, we will be less prone to shame and self-criticism.

Recent research in neuroscience tells us that there are at least three types of *emotion regulation systems* (parts of the brain that work together to control and maintain our emotions). These help us achieve our key goals in life.[1] In this chapter, we are going to look at the three emotion regulation systems in some detail, but briefly they can be summarized as the *threat system*, designed to help us detect and respond to threats in our lives; the *drive and resource acquisition system*, designed to help us to detect, be interested in, and take pleasure from securing important resources, enabling us to survive and prosper; and the *contentment and soothing system*, designed to help calm and balance the other two systems, giving us positive feelings of peaceful well-being and contentment. These three systems are represented in diagram 1: the threat system is represented by the bottom circle; the drive and resource acquisition system is represented by the left circle, and the contentment and soothing system is represented by the right circle.

---

1   If you struggle with self-confidence, it is likely that you'll have problems with your social goals, which might include developing friendships and intimate relationships, taking leadership roles, becoming a parent, and being valued by others.

Although these emotion regulation systems are represented by three distinct circles in diagram 1, it is important to see them as continuously interacting and creating patterns in our brains. This process is represented by the arrows in the diagram. A closer examination of these systems will help you understand how your emotions work, how they relate to each other, and how you can help them work in a way that will allow you to build your self-confidence.

Three Types of Affect Regulation Systems

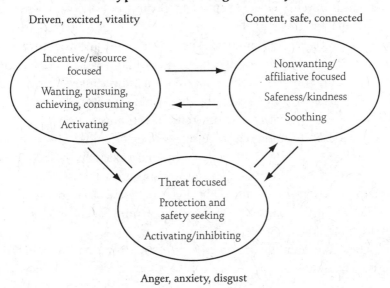

Driven, excited, vitality

Content, safe, connected

Incentive/resource focused

Wanting, pursuing, achieving, consuming

Activating

Nonwanting/ affiliative focused

Safeness/kindness

Soothing

Threat focused

Protection and safety seeking

Activating/inhibiting

Anger, anxiety, disgust

Diagram 1: Three types of emotion regulation systems

Reprinted with permission from P. Gilbert, *The Compassionate Mind* (London: Constable and Robinson, 2009).

The Threat System

All living creatures need to be able to detect things that may be a danger to them, and if they live in groups or have offspring, they need to be able to detect potential danger to others too. Our threat system is therefore a rapid-response center, the first port of call for all incoming information and the system by which such information is assessed. It acts like a customs service or passport control system—only a million times faster!

The human brain, like those of other animals, has a set menu of responses that are ready to be triggered. Our three major threat-based emotions are anxiety, anger, and disgust. These are typically linked to a range of different behaviors: to freeze or run away if we're anxious; to fight or try harder if we're angry; to turn away or get rid of something if we feel disgusted by it. It's easy to illustrate how quickly the threat system can be activated in us. Imagine that you are driving down a road when a cyclist suddenly appears right in front of you. There's not much time for thought. There is, however, a sudden punch in your stomach and a rush of anxiety. Alternatively, imagine you open your exam results and see an unexpected F. You will immediately feel a surge of anxiety and distress. Finally, imagine you are rushing to get to work and you misplace your keys or the driveway is blocked. You will probably feel overcome with panic, frustration, and anger.

In addition to initiating these surges of emotion, the threat system also changes the way your body works. For example, it will act to narrow and focus your attention in a crisis and will push you toward certain behaviors (classically flight, fight, or freeze) in response. All of this is, of course, completely automatic, not your fault, and part of the brain's basic design.

There are four important aspects of this threat system that you need to be aware of.

OVERESTIMATION OF THREAT

Imagine you are trekking through the jungle and something catches your eye. The threat system will immediately respond, directing your attention to potential danger and sending a surge of anxiety through you. Your brain tells you it could be a predator. Nine times out of ten, it probably isn't, but the fact is that you can't afford to ignore the possibility. This is called *better-safe-than-sorry* processing, because your brain is actually set up to overestimate threats and dangers in certain situations. We are, in fact, born to be irrational, and we tend to overreact because our brains are designed that way.

To add insult to injury, for many people the threat system becomes even more supercharged or superprotective. It's like having a smoke detector going off every time you cook a boiled egg or the burglar alarm ringing every time a spider moves in your house. This supercharged system is often a consequence of having lived through difficult experiences in childhood or in later years.

OVERRULING OF THE POSITIVE

Another aspect of the threat system is its tendency to overrule positive feelings and events, making us focus instead on threats and negatives. Once again, imagine you are trekking through the jungle, and this time the thing that has caught your eye is a lion. Your predesigned set of responses may quickly determine that running is the best option. As you run, you see a wonderful tree bursting with fruit next to a river jumping with fish. Such things could feed your family for months, but if you stay around to stock up, you are likely to become the lion's dinner. Alternatively, you may not even notice the tree and the river, as your attention is focused on running as fast as you can to save yourself.

In real life, we are very rarely, if ever, chased by lions—well, not around here, anyway!—but imagine walking into a room that is full of people. Nineteen out of the twenty present may look your way and smile, while one person may look over with a slightly narrowed gaze and a seemingly judgmental expression. Bang! Your attention is instantly focused on that one person, you experience a rush of anxiety or anger, and you find it difficult to engage with the more welcoming people around you. This is your better-safe-than-sorry factory setting at play, but what about all the people who were seemingly giving you a warm welcome? One of them could be your future best friend; another could be a potential partner. Unfortunately, you are not looking at them; your attention is on the only person who seems to be judging you, and you are overruling the positive.

Similarly, you might have had the experience of receiving one piece of negative feedback in a sea of positive comments. Again, it is likely that your attention will go straight to the negative comment, and you will worry about it rather than focus on all the positives.

RUMINATION AND WORRY

A third aspect of the threat system is its tendency to make you ruminate on and worry about the negative.[2] For example, say it's Christmas and you go shopping. In nine out of ten shops, the sales-people are extremely helpful and you find presents that are even better than the ones you had hoped to buy. You come away feeling really pleased. Then you visit one final shop. The clerk there makes you wait while she talks to a friend, looks at you as if you were dragged through a hedge backward, shows very little interest in helping you, sells you something that you don't really want, and shortchanges you. So whom do you talk about when you get home? You rant about that one unhelp-ful person who needs to be taught the rudiments of common courtesy.

Alternatively, you may be planning a social gathering and inviting people you care about, some of whom you haven't seen in years. But instead of looking forward to it, you spend your time worrying whether your guests will come, about what food and drink you will serve, about whether you will be ready on time, and about what the weather will be like on the day.

SIMULTANEOUS REACTIONS PULLING US IN DIFFERENT DIRECTIONS

Finally, in looking at how the threat system works, it is helpful to reflect on how simultaneous reactions can pull us in different direc-tions. Imagine your boss criticizes your efforts. What emotions do you feel? It may be anger associated with such thoughts as *How dare you criticize my work? What do you know anyway?* You may have thoughts and mental images of shouting back, punching him, or taking your revenge at a later date. Meanwhile, there may be another part of you that feels panic and thinks, *My work isn't good enough.* Part of you may want to run away, hand in your notice, or cry. In any given situation,

---

2   We human beings have an ability to go over and over things in our minds. Depending upon what we focus on, this tendency can be associated with difficult emotions. When we *ruminate*, the focus is on things that have already happened. When we *worry*, we focus on things that may happen.

quite different and conflicting emotions and behaviors can pull us in different directions.

Just when you may be thinking this is already complicated enough, the two parts of you can often react against each other. The anxious part of you may worry that your anger will get you fired while the angry part of you thinks you are being pathetic for wanting to run away, hand in your notice, or cry. At times, this sense of internal conflict may be delayed. For example, you may be quite submissive in a stressful situation but then wake up in the middle of the night, thinking *Why didn't I say X? Why did I let her get away with it?* Or you may act angrily in a situation and then, at a later date, think, *Oh, no, I shouldn't have gotten angry. I've really blown it now.* It's very common for one event to result in two very different sets of emotions, behaviors, and so forth, and these may well conflict with each other.

Of course, all this means that we have a lot to contend with. It's ironic that the system set up to help us survive is exactly the same system that can make life so difficult for us.

As you will see, helping the threat system to operate more smoothly is easier said than done, but, importantly, it is possible. The threat system often undermines us and can affect our self-confidence. The goal is to work toward recognizing when your threat system has been triggered and, when appropriate, aim to calm it down. Your responsibility is to let it do its job correctly and not let it run the show.

The Drive and Resource Acquisition System

To survive and reproduce, animals have to do a lot more than avoid danger. They have to find food and shelter and, of course, mates. They need to be motivated to go out and look for things and take pleasure in doing, achieving, and acquiring.

The drive and resource acquisition system is linked to a chemical in the brain called dopamine. This is the hormone that gives us a pleasurable buzz when we achieve things. Sometimes it's a very big buzz indeed. Imagine you had just won the lottery. Assuming you're not already a millionaire, chances are you'd have so much dopamine in your system in reaction to the astonishing news that you would be unable to sleep all night. You would be extremely excited, your head

would be full of all kinds of thoughts and ideas, you'd find it difficult
to wipe the smile off your face, and it would certainly be a while before
you'd be able to settle down and watch a movie with full concentration.
This is your drive and resource acquisition system at play.

A system that helps us enjoy what we achieve is a good thing unless
we become overfocused on achievement to the detriment of other things.
For example, many people who suffer with their self-confidence find
that they seek achievement as an antidote to feeling inadequate, threat-
ened, and vulnerable. Achievement, as well as the positive response
that it draws from others, gives them a temporary buzz and sense of self-
worth. But when they are unable to keep on achieving, maybe because
of age, strong competition, illness, or injury, problems can arise. Their
primary means for feeling good is gone, leaving a vacuum.

Some researchers, such as Jean Twenge, are concerned that modern
society intentionally overstimulates the drive and acquisition system,
supercharging it, so that we end up wanting more and more—more
excitement, more things to do, more things to acquire—and are never
quite satisfied. Powerful advertising tells us that we need more exciting
computer games, faster cars, quicker telephones. It also tells us how to
achieve better bodies, better skin, or better hair, stimulating our threat
system with such language as "dull, lifeless hair" or "fine lines and
wrinkles." This drives us to acquire a product or service that seemingly
is the answer to all the problems that have been pointed out to us. The
acquisition itself gives us a buzz even if it does not give us full-bodied
hair and a wrinkle-free face!

Much of present-day advertising is focused on giving us little dopamine rushes, which act to stimulate our drive and resource acquisition
system. The problem is that this is not the system that leads us to feel
the sense of safeness and security that is fundamental to our well-being.
In addition, it's not a system that really builds self-confidence, because
if we are driven constantly to acquire, do, and achieve, the moment we
find ourselves struggling or thinking that we're not going to achieve
something, our self-confidence collapses.

Thankfully, there is something else that enables us to feel okay
about ourselves, even when things are going badly. This is the second
secret to building self-confidence—self-compassion—which is based on
a very different type of emotion regulation system.

The Contentment and Soothing System

Animals enter a state of contentment and peacefulness when they have achieved what they need to achieve. This is usually when they are in a position of safety and are unlikely to come under attack. This state of contentment seems to be related to the chemicals in our brains called endorphins. It helps to promote a sense of peaceful contentment, for while it is being accessed, the threat and drive systems are switched off.

When considering the primary function of the contentment and soothing system, you should bear in mind that it evolved in humans over many thousands of years, primarily as a consequence of the strong bond that exists between parent and infant. In evolutionary terms, this bond serves to increase the chances of the survival of the species. The contentment and soothing system became central to what we call *attachment* and *affiliation*. Basically, the presence of the primary care-giver, more usually the mother, has a calming effect on the infant, and this is beneficial for both mother and infant.

Imagine, for example, what happens when a bird flies back to feed her fledglings and sit on the nest. They become soothed and quiet. And recall the way baby penguins sit on their father's feet, cuddling up and staying calm and content. They become distressed only if they lose contact with their parent. This is true of human babies too. A child can be relatively calm and content until the mother or caring parent suddenly vanishes, and then the child instantly becomes very distressed.

When a child's threat system is activated, and it shows distress and anxiety, what is the thing that will calm it down and turn off the threat system? The presence of the caring parent, of course. So evolution has created a situation where the kindness and care of others has a major impact on the regulation of our threat system, and all of this does not suddenly stop when we become adults. In fact, many scientific studies have shown that when we feel we are in caring contact with others, we are better able to deal with stress. So from the day that you're born to the day that you die, the kindness, helpfulness, and caring of others will have a huge impact on the quality of your life.

It's now known that when we are born our brains contain approximately 100 billion neurons, or brain cells. As we grow, the brain develops very fast. Indeed, at birth it is estimated that each neuron has approximately 2,500 connections with other neurons. By the age of two or three years, each neuron has approximately 15,000 connections to other neurons. In our early years, connections that are used infrequently or not at all disappear, while those that are regularly used multiply. So the connections that are developed and strengthened are dependent upon the experiences the baby has. If these inputs are associated with kindness, warmth, and helpfulness, which serve to soothe or calm the threat system, this is what gets laid down in the baby's brain.

Later in life, young adults learn to use those connections to help accept and experience positive emotions from others, such as the wider family, peers, coworkers, and partners. Young adults also learn how to self-soothe, to calm and reassure themselves and express self-empathy when difficult things happen.

Unfortunately, if early experiences are not particularly soothing or are actually threatening, then such positive connections may remain underdeveloped in the baby's brain. The threat system, by contrast, may become strengthened. Consequently, in adulthood we may find it difficult to accept and experience positive emotions in response to others and may be more sensitive to and perceive more threat in the environment. We may be less able to self-soothe and therefore find it difficult to recover from life's setbacks.

It is important to stress two things at this point. First, if you think that your contentment and soothing system is underdeveloped, it does not necessarily mean that your parents or caregivers are responsible for this. For example, some children are born with a tendency to like lots of cuddles and can be easily soothed, whereas others may not be born this way. Growing up, we can be affected by our siblings and peers, physical health problems, looking or being different in some way, and by all manner of other things that affect our experience of relationships and how we feel. It's true that the human brain's development is strongly influenced by our relationships with others and whether those relationships go well or badly. All of this has an effect on the kind of brain we end up with.

A second important point to stress here is that it is never too late to change things. At any point in life, we can develop or strengthen our contentment and soothing system to help regulate our threat and drive system. The key is to try to balance the systems.

CREATING AND MAINTAINING BALANCE: PHYSIOTHERAPY FOR THE BRAIN

If you wished to learn to play the piano, you would put your efforts into learning the keyboard, and your brain would develop accordingly. In other words, new neurons and new connections would make it possible to achieve your ambition. (Yes, even adults make new connections and new neurons on a daily basis.) For some, it might be a difficult journey but one that would be ultimately worthwhile. For others, it might be an enjoyable process. Similarly, if we want to enhance or maintain our well-being and self-confidence, we need to apply ourselves to it. This effort can actually change our brains and the way our minds work.

Because of this, the compassionate-mind approach often refers to this work as *physiotherapy for the brain*. However, instead of building muscle, these exercises build new neural networks and pathways within the brain. Through such efforts, we are able to strengthen our ability to feel different and become more content, secure, and self-confident. Once we have developed this ability, we can then work to maintain or even increase it.

CONCLUSIONS

This chapter introduced the concept of emotion regulation systems to help you understand your emotional makeup a little better. Hopefully you will now be able to recognize that, as human beings, it is very easy for our very complex threat system to run the show. We can also get caught up in feeding our drive and resource acquisition system, and at times this can be to our own detriment. Our contentment and soothing system and its ability to balance the other two systems, keeping them in check, is key to our mental well-being.

Thankfully, neurogenesis and neuroplasticity mean that we can change our brains and build our self-confidence. Chapter 3 will consider the typical traps we often fall into that may end up undermining our self-confidence, and it will look again at how focusing on compassion can help.

Finally, standing back from the chapter as a whole, it may help you to make a few personal observations in your journal or notebook. These may take the form of things you wish to remember or questions that this material has raised in your mind. The answers to these should become clearer as you read the rest of the book and work through the exercises it contains.

3

How and Why We Undermine Ourselves and How Compassion Can Help

We have to learn to be our own best friends because we fall
too easily into the trap of being our own worst enemies.

—Roderick Thorp

We human beings have a whole range of ways in which we can undermine our own self-confidence. You may be able to identify with each of these to a greater or lesser extent. However, as people vary in the degree to which they undermine themselves, so too does the toll this takes. The biggest culprits for self-undermining are shame, overstriving and perfectionism, and self-criticism.

Too Much vs. Too Little Information

For some people, the detail the book goes into here will be exactly what they need to truly understand themselves better. Others may find this wealth of information counterproductive, especially when they wish to start "doing" something. It is worth noting, however, that understanding ourselves is a key part of doing, as it helps counteract some of the ways in which we habitually undermine ourselves.

Those who would like more information on shame and self-undermining than is outlined in this chapter will find further reading in the resources at the back of the book.

This chapter will look at how we habitually undermine ourselves in these three ways. Simply being able to recognize these habits in yourself can be a huge step toward addressing them and changing things for the better.

At the end, this chapter will look at how focusing on self-compassion instead of self-criticism can help build self-confidence.

HOW SHAME UNDERMINES OUR SELF-CONFIDENCE

Shame can prevent us from building our self-confidence because it rarely, if ever, allows us to let people in. We may hide behind a mask or an image we wish to portray to others, and this decreases the likelihood of our ever receiving the validation we need. It is therefore helpful to carefully examine shame in all its guises.

The Power of Shame

Most of us have a sense of what we mean by *shame*. It is related to feeling bad about ourselves and in some way feeling that other people see us as inadequate, inferior, or incompetent. To help you understand the extent to which shame can affect you, try the brief exercise below.

Exercise 1: How Shame Affects
Your Mind and Body

Just for a moment, think back to a time when you felt ashamed. Try not to bring to mind anything too major; the point is simply to touch briefly on the feeling.

Once you have managed to connect with that experience of shame, spend a little time asking yourself the following questions. If you find them difficult to answer, briefly revisit the memory and try once more to give some answers.

1. How did shame feel in your body? For example, did you notice a sensation as if your heart were sinking, or did you notice an unusual feeling in your stomach? Did you feel hot or maybe experience an increase in your heart rate?

2. What thoughts went through your mind about yourself and about what other people might be thinking of you?

3. What emotions did you feel? Perhaps you felt anxious or angry, maybe confused or simply paralyzed, finding it difficult to think or feel anything.

4. What did you want to do? Did you want to run away, curl into a ball, or lash out?

Now, having answered each of these questions, take a few minutes to let the experience fade from your mind and body.[1]

---

1   If a feeling of unease or heightened emotion remains after you have carried out this exercise or any other exercise in the book, it may be helpful to recall a recent time when you have felt content and comfortable, perhaps on your own or when you were with someone else, and let this image fill your mind and body.

This exercise will make you more aware of how the experience of shame can result in a whole array of reactions. These include physical sensations, certain types of emotions and thoughts, and the urge to react in various ways. Shame typically involves feeling exposed in some way, paired with the experience of feeling flawed, inadequate, or bad.

Often shame silences us. Our head goes down and we want to creep away and stay in the background. However, this is not always the case. Sometimes when people feel shame, rather than feeling inferior and submissive, they can react with aggression and feel the urge to fight back. Although we are not going to explore the problem of anger specifically here, those who identify with this may want to read Russell Kolts's book from this series, *The Compassionate-Mind Guide to Managing Your Anger* (see resources).

Understanding how shame works in us and what we can do about it is a very important step on the way to developing self-confidence. Compassion-focused therapist Paul Gilbert, who has spent a long time researching shame, points out that shame has three types of focus. He has named these *reflected shame*, *external shame*, and *internal shame*. As you will see, it is likely that internal and external shame are most closely associated with the undermining of self-confidence. For this reason, this book will focus most strongly on these two categories of shame.

The Origins of Compassion-Focused Therapy

CFT was originally developed specifically for people who experience high levels of shame. Therapists and researchers, as well as those experiencing such difficulties, had observed that more traditional forms of therapy were not meeting their needs. People who experience shame have often experienced a number of difficulties in their early lives, maybe in the family context or at school. It is understandable that, given such experiences, it can be difficult for people to feel safe in the world, safe in the therapy, or even to like themselves much. This can impact on an individual's efforts to build self-confidence.

Reflected Shame

Reflected shame is what we may feel in response to other people's actions; it is not about us directly. Alternatively, reflected shame is the shame other people feel because of our actions. For example, we may feel reflected shame because a member of our family has done a particular thing that is deemed shameful. Jasvinder Sanghera has looked at this form of shame within certain cultural communities. In her book *Shame*, Jasvinder drew on her own background and explored the experiences of a subsection of Asian women who are forced into arranged marriages. The experience of reflected shame can be so serious in some cultures that it may lead to so-called honor killing of those deemed to have brought shame on their families.

The experience of reflected shame can also be less serious and border more on embarrassment, especially after some time has elapsed. Many parents will squirm when their child points out something about another person (usually within earshot), such as the person's size, hair color, wrinkles, or any other characteristic. We may apologize, raise our eyes, or laugh awkwardly, but even when we know the words were totally innocent, we feel reflected shame at that moment as though our child's actions are a reflection on us. It's only later, when the shame has turned into embarrassment, that we may be able to laugh at the situation with a friend or partner.

Alternatively, for those with a dog, reflected shame may be the experience you have when it decides to go to the toilet in an inappropriate place or sniffs another dog where you know it will (but wish it wouldn't). It is amazing how, at that moment, we can feel shame about what our dog is doing, as if his behavior were a reflection on us!

Reflected shame serves a number of functions. If you wish to study this area further, you may wish to read Jasvinder Sanghera's book or a number of titles by Paul Gilbert. More information can be found in the resources section at the back of this book.

External Shame

External shame is associated with the idea that other people are thinking negatively about us. Maybe your boss criticizes your work and you feel belittled in his or her eyes. Maybe if you have put on weight—or because of some other aspect of your appearance—you think other people are judging you negatively.

Upon feeling that someone is viewing us negatively, we may alter our behavior. For example, we may become very submissive at work or even stop going out. We may dress to disguise a perceived flaw, become overly apologetic, or maybe lash out. External shame is the sense we have of how we exist in the minds of others, and some of us worry about this a great deal. The more we worry about the way other people judge us and feel about us, the more this can work to undermine our own self-confidence.

But why do we worry about what other people feel and think about us? Well, there are a couple of very good reasons.

First, in order for our contentment and soothing system (see chapter 2) to develop, we need the kindness and caring of others. We also need to make judgments, initially basic but later more complex, about who is safe and who is not. Human beings have a built-in mechanism that motivates us to look at others and wonder, *What are they thinking about or feeling toward me?* and, ultimately, *Whom can I trust?* In childhood and into adulthood, we hopefully develop the capacity to *self-regulate*, to soothe or reassure ourselves in the face of life's setbacks. This obviously helps us to secure our place in the world, but it is still vitally important for us to be able to think about what is going on in the minds of other people.

Our ability to cope with external shame, or the possibility that others may not think as highly of us as we'd like them to, often comes down to our own self-confidence and ability to self-regulate. In summary, we human beings are predestined to spend time trying to work out what other people think of us. If we have had difficult experiences, usually in childhood but maybe afterward, we are more sensitive to threat from others. Working to develop our contentment and soothing system can help us regulate or tone down this sense of threat, but it can also give us self-confidence in our ability to deal with difficult situations. The more self-confident we feel within ourselves, the easier it is to cope when things aren't quite as we would like them to be.

Secondly, Paul Gilbert points out that the experience of external shame alerts us to the possibility of being rejected in some way. It also potentially guides us to behave in ways that may make it more likely for us to be accepted and protected by those around us. If others see us negatively, then they are less likely to be our friends, want to interact with us, or support us when times are hard. If, on the other hand, they feel good about us and like us, then it is more likely they will want to be our friends and help us. So, in a way, external shame warns us about how we exist in the minds of others, which has had important implications, initially for our survival and in more recent times for our well-being.

Humans are highly motivated to seek the praise and approval of others and have an inherent need to belong and to share. Consequently, it really hurts if we feel there are things about us that will devalue us in other people's eyes or detract from our endeavors.

It is important to recognize that we all like to feel valued and wanted by those around us. There is no shame in this. It is a deep-rooted trait that has proved highly significant in evolutionary terms. Approval from others helps us feel safe in the world: part of the group. However, if we feel bad about ourselves, we may feel under more scrutiny from others and perceive more social threat than is warranted, and this, in turn, may mean that we overstrive to be accepted. As you will see later, this overstriving can itself cause us problems.

Internal Shame

The final kind of shame is internal, where our attention is fixed upon ourselves, or how we think and feel about ourselves. Sometimes there may be consistency between what other people seem to feel and think about us and how we view ourselves, while at other times people may be very complimentary to us, while our own judgments are much more negative.

For example, if we are subtly bullied in our social group and the butt of many jokes, we can start to think that what people are saying is true and begin to feel the same way about ourselves. As a result, we may feel both external and internal shame. However, in another scenario, we may find that despite everyone commenting favorably on our work and stating that we are a good friend or partner, we feel different about ourselves. We still feel internal shame, as though there were something wrong with us. Then, because what people say is inconsistent with how we view ourselves, we may start thinking *They're only saying that!* or *If they really knew me, they wouldn't like me. They are lulling me into a false sense of security.*

There's nothing that undermines self-confidence more than internal shame. One of the most important aspects of internal shame is self-criticism, which will be discussed later in this chapter.

But whether it is reflected, external, or internal shame, or a blend of all three, shame undermines our self-confidence because while suffering from it we rarely, if ever, let others see the true person underneath. We hide behind an image we wish to promote to others and so decrease the likelihood of our ever being valued for the person we really are. It is like building a house with no foundation; we may achieve great things, but we constantly undermine our own success by attributing it not to ourselves but to other factors. The resulting feeling of instability is like living permanently with the threat of our houses falling down around our ears.

HOW OVERSTRIVING AND PERFECTIONISM CAN UNDERMINE OUR SELF-CONFIDENCE

This next section will look at overstriving and perfectionism. As you will see, these two areas overlap with those outlined above. However, in an effort to understand and therefore be kinder to yourself, it can be helpful to consider different ways of viewing things in the hope that something will resonate for you.

Overstriving

One way in which we often try to deal with external shame is to try to prove ourselves to other people. Psychologists have researched how this desire to prove ourselves can instead undermine our self-confidence.

Over fifty years ago, researchers into human motivation pointed out that we can be motivated to achieve things in different ways. We may be *value achievers* or *need achievers*.

VALUE ACHIEVERS

People in this group derive pleasure from doing things because they feel value in the achievement itself. This may include swimming a mile, climbing a mountain, passing exams, or taking up a particular career. Even small achievements give them pleasure.

NEED ACHIEVERS

This group, who seem similarly motivated to swim the mile, climb the mountain, pass exams, and so on, seem to derive less pleasure from the achievement itself. By contrast, they derive pleasure mostly from the applause, approval, and accolades that accompany the achievement. Indeed, if the activity does not bring any such accolades or approval, they quickly stop doing it. These people thus need achievement as a means of gaining approval and feeling valued by others. Notice how value achievers and need achievers can outwardly look quite similar though they are not.

It is important that we start to think carefully about our goals and values and why we do exactly what we do. There is nothing wrong with being a need achiever and wanting the approval of others, but we've got to be careful, as this approach to life can leave us open to disappointment, is less predictable, and can work to undermine our self-confidence. Of course, most of us are a blend of value and need achievers, but people who struggle with self-confidence tend to be more on the need-achiever side of things.

In time, researchers looked at motivation in slightly different ways. Benjamin Dykman, for example, suggested there are two main motivations behind achievement: *growth seeking* and *validation seeking.*

GROWTH SEEKING

Growth seekers enjoy challenges and their ability to learn. As such, they mature through learning from their mistakes. If you have this attitude to life, then very clearly you're going to be continually building your self-confidence because you are going to be learning how to deal with mistakes and constantly getting better at things.

VALIDATION SEEKING

Dykman used the term *validation seekers* to describe individuals who feel under constant pressure to prove themselves as likable and acceptable to others, suggesting that validation seeking develops in children when they are constantly uncertain of being loved and valued. Alternatively, validation seekers may come from families where others were perfectionists and much was expected of them. We can see how this scenario developed for Kelly.

•   *Kelly's Story*

Kelly came from a family where both parents were quite demanding and critical of her. She constantly felt she had to live up to their expectations and prove herself to them. They were not unkind to her, nor were they lacking in some degree of affection though they were undemonstrative.

Kelly grew up with a sense of needing constantly to strive to prove herself and a nagging sense of not being good enough. In fact, she reported that she felt okay with herself only when she had succeeded at something that other people placed value on (and even this was short-lived). Although to others her self-confidence seemed adequate, in certain areas it was actually quite fragile, as Kelly felt everything could come tumbling down around her at any moment if she took her eye off the ball.

Perfectionism

Although perfectionism can be helpful at certain times and in certain aspects of our lives, it can also undermine our self-confidence.

In a series of studies, psychologist David Dunkley and colleagues demonstrated that there are at least two types of perfectionism that look the same but are very different: having high standards for the sake of the standards themselves and having high standards for the sake of "evaluative concerns."

HIGH STANDARDS FOR THE SAKE OF THE STANDARDS THEMSELVES

You want someone with this type of perfectionism to be your brain surgeon. Such perfectionists are very careful and have exacting standards. They are highly motivated and gain pleasure from perfection itself.

HIGH STANDARDS FOR THE SAKE OF EVALUATIVE CONCERNS

Having high standards for the sake of evaluative concerns means being frightened of making mistakes, frightened of rejection, and frightened of being shamed. Dunkley and colleagues found that people who were perfectionists because they were concerned about what other people thought were much more vulnerable to all kinds of mental health difficulties.[2]

It's not just as a consequence of our family environment that such fears or concerns arise. Children who are vulnerable to bullying or feeling marginalized at school because, for example, they are not good at sports or because they look a certain way can sometimes develop this great need to prove themselves.

If we wish to build our self-confidence, it is helpful for us to stop trying to prove ourselves and instead make active choices about the changes it may be helpful for us to make. While wanting to prove ourselves to others—and to be approved of—is absolutely essential to being human (imagine people who didn't care about what other people thought of them), the most important thing is to achieve balance. If the balance swings too far in favor of needing to prove yourself, rather than enjoying your achievements and learning from your mistakes, you will get into difficulties. High levels of fear or concern about what other

---

2   Paul Gilbert and colleagues have also looked at the link between such factors and mental health problems and have shown that when we strive to avoid inferiority (which is different from seeking superiority), we often do so because we are frightened of being excluded and rejected. This, in turn, sets us up for problems with anxiety and depression.

people might think can lead to all kinds of difficulties, from shyness to social anxiety to depression.

Lynne Henderson has written a book on shyness and social anxiety in the Compassionate Mind series; see the resources section if this seems to be a particular problem for you. In her book, Henderson deals primarily with social confidence, whereas the book you are reading is looking more at self-confidence.

HOW SELF-CRITICISM UNDERMINES OUR SELF-CONFIDENCE

Self-criticism is easy to misunderstand. At times it can be helpful. At other times it can undermine our self-confidence. The key to understanding whether it is helpful for you is to notice the emotions and motivations that accompany it. To help explore what emotions and motivations are associated with your own self-criticism, grab a pen or pencil and your notebook or journal and work through exercise 2. This exercise may be associated with difficult emotions, so you may wish to try it only briefly.

Exercise 2: Identifying Your Self-Critic

Think back to a recent occasion when you were critical of yourself and your efforts—nothing too major because you just want to glimpse the critical part of yourself. The situation may focus on something you found difficult at work, a time when you lost your keys or wallet, or when you made a mistake.

Once you are able to bring a situation to mind, imagine that the self-critical part of you could be viewed as a person. Now answer the following questions, using the space provided or your notebook.

Exercise 2, Part 1

1. If your self-critical thoughts took on the appearance of an actual person, what would that person look like?

2. What would the person's facial expression be?

3. Is he or she physically big or small in comparison to you?

4. What is the person's tone of voice like?

5. If you can imagine a body, what is the posture and body like?

6. What emotions is this person directing your way?

7. Does he or she remind you of anyone?

Exercise 2, Part 2

Now that you've completed the imagery part of this exercise, it's time for reflection. What have you discovered?

Having gone through each part, take a few minutes to let the experience fade from your mind and body.

Often when we look in detail at the self-critical part of ourselves, we find that it is associated with feelings of frustration, contempt, and anger. We may find that the self-critical part is either a figure that looms large or a little gremlin that wags its finger in constant reproof. Often its tone of voice is hostile. This exercise may evoke memories or images of someone from the past, someone who was critical of you and your efforts.

For many people, the previous exercise illustrates that their own self-critic is a bully. The image they generate may be someone from the past or an amalgamation of people. Others realize that such a critic is unlikely to be helpful to them, as they actually feel immobilized in its presence.

Why We Engage in Self-Criticism

To understand why we engage in self-criticism, try the next exercise.

Exercise 3: Recognizing Your Fears about Letting Go of Self-Criticism

For a moment, just imagine that you could take away your self-criticism.

1. What are your greatest fears about giving up your self-criticism?

2. What do you think might happen if you let it go?

3. When you look at your self-critic and see the emotions coming back to you from it, to what extent do you think it genuinely has your best interests at heart?

4. Does it really care about you and take great joy in seeing you flourish, do well, and be happy?

5. If your self-critic does have your best interests at heart, is it going about things in the right way?

6. What have you discovered?

Having answered each of the questions, take a few minutes to let the experience fade from your mind and body.

You may fear letting go of your self-criticism, yet it is probably tinged with frustration and disappointment, anger, or even contempt. As such, your self-criticism is probably not the best part of you to help build your self-confidence. In actual fact, it is more likely to drag you down and undermine both you and your efforts.

Learning from mistakes is very important, but we have a much better chance of doing this and doing it in a sustained way if we go about it by building and nurturing our self-confidence rather than undermining ourselves with self-criticism, frustration, and contempt.

The following exercise illustrates this point further.

Exercise 4: Choosing a Guide in Building Your Self-Confidence

Read the following scenario and imagine yourself in it:

You have a child for whom you care greatly. When you enroll your child at school, there are two classes for her age group, so you have a choice between two teachers. You visit one class and the first teacher tells you she is going to help the children improve by acting quickly to correct their mistakes. This will result in, for example, having something taken away from them or having them sit at the front of the class so that they learn not to make the same mistake twice. While the teacher is relaying this information to you, a child in the class spills a drink across the table and on the floor. Immediately the teacher notices and shouts at her in a stern voice to be more careful, telling her to clean up the mess she has made and never to be so clumsy again. To reinforce this message, the child is given twenty lines to write out. The teacher whispers in your ear: "If they learn that bad things happen after mistakes, they quickly learn not to make them."

On leaving, you go straight to the other class. The second teacher tells you that he feels it is very important for children to profit by their mistakes, be open about them and curious about how they came about, and learn how they can prevent them in the future. As you are speaking, a child's knife and fork clatter to the floor (both visits were occurring at lunchtime!). The second teacher quickly approaches the child, squats down next to him, and in a gentle and inquisitive voice says, "What happened?" "I was putting my hand up for second helpings, and my elbow caught my knife, and that caught my fork, and..." "John, given that this happened, what do you need to remember the next time you want to put your hand up for seconds?" And so the conversation between child and teacher continues for a little while in this gentle manner.

Which teacher would you choose for your child?

If the answer is the second teacher, then why are you always sending yourself to the first?

Having answered these questions, take a few minutes to let the impact of the experience fade from your mind.

You may decide that making such choices is easy when things are going relatively well, but what about when things are difficult and you need to have courage? In answer to this, briefly imagine that you are going into a burning house. Whom would you like to give you cover and support as you go in? Someone who is reassuring and encouraging or someone who is quick to criticize and shout (making you more anxious) when you get into difficulties? It's a no-brainer.

When things get tough, you need a friend by your side. This is basically the essence of compassion-focused therapy. We build self-confidence by learning how to become a good friend to ourselves. This means being neither too critical (or, in extreme cases, tearing ourselves to bits) nor too passive, always saying "There, there...poor you."

A good friend will have your best interests at heart. He or she will be sympathetic to all that life throws at you but will encourage you and be your cheerleader when you have something you need to face. Indeed, what you are going to do throughout this book is learn how to develop self-compassion, which brings support and encouragement, together with such qualities as strength, empathy, and nonjudgment.

Paul Gilbert, in his book *The Compassionate Mind*, makes the distinction between shame-based self-criticism (maybe what we do at the moment) and compassionate self-correction and uses the following table to help us compare the two.

Distinguishing between Shame-Based Self-Criticism and Compassionate Self-Correction

Shame-Based Self-Criticism	Compassionate Self-Correction
• Focuses on the desire to condemn and punish	• Focuses on the desire to improve
• Punishes past errors and is often backward looking	• Emphasizes growth and enhancement
• Is given with anger, frustration contempt, disappointment	• Is forward looking
• Concentrates on deficits and fear of exposure	• Is given with encouragement, support, kindness
• Focuses on a global sense of self	• Builds on positives (seeing what you did well and then considering learning points)
• Includes a high fear of failure	• Focuses on attributes and specific qualities of self
• Increases chances of avoidance and withdrawal	• Emphasizes hope for success
	• Increases the chances of engaging

Consider example of critical teacher with a child who is struggling.	Consider example of encouraging, supportive teacher with a child who is struggling.
For Transgression	*For Transgression*
• Shame, avoidance, fear	• Guilt, engaging
• Heart sinks, lowered mood	• Sorrow, remorse
• Aggression	• Reparation

Reprinted with permission from P. Gilbert, *The Compassionate Mind* (London: Constable and Robinson, 2009).

Compassionate self-correction—or the term I personally use, *compassionate self-adjustment*—wins hands down every time.

HOPE IN THE SHAPE OF THE BRAIN'S AMAZING ABILITIES

If you're still not convinced as yet of the need to address our habit of undermining ourselves and to develop self-compassion instead, hopefully the following section will consolidate the idea. The compassionate-mind approach looks at how thoughts and images can influence the way our brains and bodies work. This can be beneficial in helping us to make informed decisions or take more control over what we think and imagine.

How Our Brains Respond to Stimulus

Imagine that you are very hungry and you see a wonderful plate of food or smell amazing scents coming from the kitchen. What happens to your saliva and stomach acids? They get going, don't they? This is because the sight and smell of the food stimulate an area of your brain called the *hypothalamus*, and its job is to prepare your body for eating.

But suppose it's late at night and maybe all the shops are closed or you have no money, so you just sit and find yourself fantasizing about a lovely meal to satisfy your hunger. What happens to your saliva and stomach acids then? They get going in exactly the same way, don't they? Isn't that interesting? Just the image and the thought of food can stimulate the brain to release acids into your stomach because your brain thinks you're about to eat.

Here's another situation. What happens if you go out one night and meet someone you find really attractive? You flirt with each other, and toward the end of the evening this person leans in toward you to kiss you. In this situation, you are likely to become aroused. Signals will go straight to your brain and stimulate an area called the *pituitary gland*, which will release hormones into your body and cause arousal. But here is the important part: suppose you simply imagine all of this is happening. What happens in your body then? What's interesting is that human beings can derive arousal simply through deliberately created mental imagery. This stimulates the pituitary gland in exactly the same way as if the imaginary scenario were really happening. The point here is that the different images you create in your head can stimulate different areas in your body. When you imagine a meal, you are stimulating your hypothalamus; when you imagine things that are sexually arousing, you are stimulating your pituitary gland.

It's very clear that in these everyday situations our thoughts and mental imagery can actually have a major effect on our bodies. We all know this, of course, but often don't really see the full implications, and these are huge.

If you experience bullying at school or work, it is likely that it will activate your threat system. You may experience anxiety, anger, or sadness. You may feel the urge to fight or run, or you may freeze. You may even experience all of these feelings at once.

But what happens when, instead of being bullied by someone else, we bully and criticize ourselves, taunt ourselves with things we are unhappy with or that make us feel ashamed? What happens when we are constantly unkind, critical, and harsh toward ourselves and let our self-critical part get the upper hand and run the show? What part of the brain are we stimulating then? These thoughts, images, and memories are going to stimulate the threat system, over and over, as if these things were constantly recurring. Going back to the three-circle model presented in chapter 2, you'll see that if you continually stimulate the threat system, with certain internal thoughts, memories, and imagery, it will become out of balance.

So although it can seem that the critical part of ourselves has our best interests at heart, it actually stimulates the threat system over and over again. This then triggers a further layer of emotions, narrowing our attention and predisposing us toward predesigned responses such as fight, flight, or freeze. How can this scenario ever build self-confidence? It can only undermine it.

You Can Change What You Tell Yourself

As seen previously, if we grow up in and experience a nurturing environment, we are more likely to feel a sense of contentment. But what happens if we learn how to be kinder and more supportive to ourselves? In this new frame of mind, what would happen if we tried to understand why we experienced difficulties?

Imagine what would happen if you committed yourself to really building your self-confidence by generating a friendly voice in your head that was always supportive of you. A voice that was strong and instilled courage with which to face life's difficulties. This would build and maintain your contentment and soothing system, which would help to bring emotional balance. Maybe in this mindset, you might also feel encouraged and inspired, and this would also stimulate your drive and resource acquisition system in a helpful way. Diagram 2 below helps to summarize this.

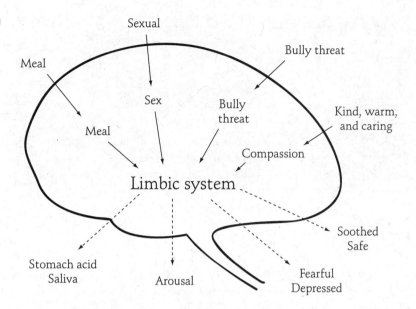

Diagram 2: How thoughts and imagery affect our brains and bodies

Reprinted with permission from P. Gilbert, *The Compassionate Mind* (London: Constable and Robinson, 2009).

How We Speak to Ourselves Is Extremely Important

From a scientific perspective, Paul Gilbert and colleagues have looked at what happens in the brain when we are kind and self-reassuring rather than self-critical. They have found evidence that self-reassurance and self-criticism stimulate quite different systems in our brains. This therefore suggests that the tone we use to speak to ourselves is very important.

CONCLUSIONS

If we can gain a greater understanding of the way our minds work and a better awareness of the traps we fall into, we can then learn to implement more helpful strategies: ones that will increase our self-confidence. Building self-confidence begins with recognizing what we're doing to ourselves, acknowledging that problems with self-confidence are not our fault but arise from the way our brains are designed, and then making a commitment to change things for the better.

The rest of this book is going to be helping you do exactly that: build your self-confidence by fostering a better relationship with yourself. Following this path will help you gain the strength and courage needed to face, engage with, and address the difficulties you may have in your life rather than avoid them.

4

Making Sense of Our Experiences

Experience is a hard teacher because she gives you
the test first, the lesson afterwards.

—Vernon Sanders Law

In chapters 1 through 3, you saw that self-confidence is something you need to build and maintain rather than something you are either born with or without. You then went on to look at self-confidence from an evolutionary perspective, with examples of the ways in which we can often undermine ourselves and therefore stunt the development of self-confidence. Finally you saw how developing compassion can help.

This chapter will present some exercises specifically designed to help you develop a compassionate understanding of your own difficulties. This will help to counteract any self-undermining and provide a platform on which to build your self-confidence. The exercises involve

- Understanding what has influenced you

- Recognizing your key concerns and fears

- Noting your coping strategies, why you may adopt them, and their unintended consequences

- Developing your own formulation

- Making sense of things

It is worth noting that undertaking the exercises within this chapter can be an emotional experience. The exercises can spotlight difficult things that have happened in the past and give rise to some troubling *shoulds, shouldn'ts,* and *if onlys.* You may find that you slip into self-criticism and feel emotions such as sadness, anger, anxiety, or shame. Later this book will give you ways of dealing with these emotions, but the first step is to understand the origins of the difficulties you may be experiencing, how they affect you, and how this in turn impacts your self-confidence.

At the end of the chapter, you will read Andy's story and look at his personal formulation. This should give you an idea of how others have gained an understanding of the influences brought to bear on them, the coping strategies they've adopted, and the unintended consequences of these strategies.

OUR INFLUENCES: NATURE AND NURTURE

Most people agree that we are the product of both nature and nurture. In other words, a combination of our biology (nature) and our experiences (nurture) influences who we are.

This can be observed in a bit more detail. First, our genes can predispose us to a certain temperament; they can give us the capacity to reach a particular level of academic or emotional intelligence. Genes influence the way we look and can predispose us to certain physical health difficulties. Second, our genes and biology are influenced and shaped by the environment we find ourselves in. This begins from the moment we are conceived and can include experiencing certain life events, such as moving schools, bereavement, and problematic relationships with our peers; influences exerted by our family environment, such as the effect brothers and sisters have on us, how we are parented, and the kind of place we live in; and society in general, such as how our culture is viewed, our sexual orientation, or our religious beliefs.

Exercise 5: Noting What Has Influenced You

An infinite number of things shape our lives, but the following worksheet lists some common ones that can be associated with difficulties with self-confidence. Some of them may apply to you; others may not. Read through the list and check off any that you recognize, or you can write in your notebook.

You may find this hard to do on your first attempt. It may be helpful to consider your life in separate periods of time and in different environments. For example, what influenced you up to the point of starting primary school? What about during periods you attended different schools? What was affecting you at home, at school, and in other areas of your life? And so forth.

It is quite likely that this list will not cover everything that has had or still has an influence on your self-confidence. After you've checked off anything that applies to you, you may add any other experiences that have affected your self-confidence.

Worksheet 1: Your Influences

____ Growing up around people who lacked self-confidence

____ Growing up around people who were seemingly good at everything when you found yourself to be less so

____ Love and affection being seemingly dependent on success

____ Being around people who were self-critical and/or critical of you

____ Experiencing little love and/or affection

____ Being naturally more introverted or shy

_____ Bereavements

_____ Loss of key friendships due to moving to a new house, changing schools, or both

_____ Having physical difficulties

_____ Unusual experiences, such as seeing or hearing things other people didn't seem to see or hear

_____ Having difficulties such as dyslexia, dyspraxia, or dyscalculia, making learning difficult

_____ Experiencing bullying or indifference from your peers or siblings

_____ Difficult relationships, including friendships or sexual relationships

_____ Traumatic events such as physical, sexual, or emotional abuse, being the victim of a crime, or being involved in some form of accident

_____ Experiencing difficult teaching styles

_____ Looking "different" from other people

_____ Issues related to your sexuality or identity

_____ Other influences: _____

_____

_____

Further Thoughts about What Influences You

Although you are currently being encouraged to reflect on difficult times, it's likely that some of your influences and experiences have been positive. These may be easy for you to recall, or they may be more difficult because of low mood or high levels of anxiety that cloud the picture. Some of us, unfortunately, may lack such positive influences and experiences.

To complicate things further, some influences and experiences associated with difficulties in self-confidence may arise from scenarios that are not obviously problematic. Here are a few examples:

- It is likely that all parents have a mixture of positive and negative influences on their children.

- Self-confident siblings can be fun to be around and can help us do things, but they can also prevent us from building self-confidence when they do everything for us. We don't learn that we can do things for ourselves.

- A very close family that does everything together may be a great environment to grow up in, but it may also mean that we have little experience of doing things outside the immediate family other than at school, and this can prevent aspects of our self-confidence from developing.

- Physical health problems may restrict us in certain areas of our lives, result in pain and discomfort, and cause other problems. However, they may result in our identifying with other people who experience similar problems and sometimes may make us feel special.

- Being a twin may be a very special experience, but it may mean we are always being judged against our sibling. For example, people may ask, "Which is the naughty one?" or "Which is the self-confident one?" and you may be labeled one or the other. Alternatively, you may have the experience of always being viewed as identical to your sibling. Being a twin can also prevent other friendships from developing.

- Being the eldest child may mean you had more time with your parents in your early years and had other advantages. Being the eldest can also mean, however, that you had to be more grown up than your siblings were when they reached the same age. With the arrival of younger siblings, you may have felt you had to share your parents more. In a similar way, being a middle or youngest child can have both pluses and minuses.

KEY CONCERNS AND FEARS

It is understandable that based on our experiences we may develop key concerns or fears. These then drive or influence our behavior, our emotions, our thinking, and our focus of attention, as well as our physiology. These concerns or fears can be separated into two categories:

Concerns and fears relating to or about our *external world*, such as what people may think of us or how they may behave toward us

Concerns and fears relating to or about our *internal world*, such as what we think about ourselves

Exercise 6: Recognizing Your Key Concerns and Fears

The following worksheet lists a number of common concerns and fears that can be linked to difficulties with self-confidence. Some of them may apply to you; others may not. Read through the list and check off the ones that you have experienced or currently identify with. Alternatively, you may wish to jot them down in your notebook.

If you have any concerns and fears that are not listed here, you can add your own thoughts. Alternatively, you might want to use different wording to describe a concern or fear that is listed here. You can use your own words to describe how it applies to you.

Things may not initially spring to mind, or it may be difficult to recall former fears and concerns because you are now in a different frame of mind. It may be helpful to spend a little time reflecting on this in the following ways:

- Think back to difficult periods in your life, maybe using what you identified in exercise 5 as a prompt.

- Think about recent occasions when you have experienced anxiety, sadness, or anger. What were the concerns or fears that were uppermost in your mind at that time?

Things That We Can Easily Fear

It is worth noting that as a consequence of our evolution, we are programmed to be wary or scared of certain harmful things, which helps to ensure the survival of the species. Fears that are quick to develop in us include a fear of heights, a fear of things that move erratically, such as spiders, and a fear of confined spaces and the dark. In addition, because we are a social species, we are also primed to be wary or scared of any degree of social threat. This may involve becoming wary when someone appears to be evaluating us negatively or looks angry. As a consequence, we constantly monitor and react to potential threats from others. This evolutionary wiring helps us to remain part of the group, from which we derive strength and protection. It is therefore not surprising that what underpins many of these feelings and concerns are fears about negative judgment from others, as this could lead to social isolation.

Worksheet 2: Your Key Concerns and Fears

Fears and concerns relating to your external world:

_____ People will think badly of you or judge you.

_____ People will behave negatively toward you (verbally, physically, etc.).

_____ You will be isolated from people.

_____ Others will reject you.

_____ Other fears and concerns: _____

_____

_____

Fears and concerns relating to your internal world:

_____ Your emotions will get the better of you or are dangerous.

_____ You will not be able to or cannot control your actions.

_____ The thoughts and mental images you have are dangerous.

_____ There is something wrong with you, physically or mentally.

_____ Other fears and concerns: _____

_____

_____

_____

COPING STRATEGIES AND THEIR CONSEQUENCES

A combination of influences and experiences can lead us to develop certain concerns and fears. It is these that can drive us toward protective or coping strategies that are meant to help us. While some strategies appear to be intentional choices, others seem more automatic. Although designed to be helpful to us, many of our actions have unfortunate consequences or drawbacks that are unintended.

Exercise 7: Noting Your Coping Strategies, Why You May Adopt Them, and Their Unintended Consequences

Read through the coping strategies listed in the following worksheet and check off those that you use. Also check off their intended function (why you use them) and their unintended consequences or drawbacks if what's listed applies to you. If there are other reasons you do certain things or other drawbacks that are not listed here, you may add this information in the space provided.

Worksheet 3: Intended Functions and Unintended Consequences of Your Coping Strategies

Coping Strategy	Intended Functions	Possible Unintended Consequences or Drawbacks
____ Being as others want	____ Avoid rejection ____ Avoid conflict ____ Keep people happy Other:	____ Feelings of resentment toward other people ____ Negating ____ Own needs are not met ____ Exhausting Other:
____ Keeping people at arm's length	____ Avoid rejection/ disappointment ____ Avoid conflict Other:	____ Isolating ____ Low mood ____ Anxiety Other:
____ Always putting on a happy or brave face/wearing a mask	____ Avoid rejection/ disappointment Other:	____ Exhausting ____ No one knows the true you ____ Prevents a feeling of true acceptance from others Other:

Coping Strategy	Intended Functions	Possible Unintended Consequences or Drawbacks
____ Deferring or relying on others	____ Avoid failure ____ Avoid anxiety Other:	____ Feelings of resentment ____ Prevent own skills from developing Other:
____ Settling for things that are not ideal; making do	____ Prevent disappointment Other:	____ Resentment ____ Conflict ____ Things become mediocre Other:
____ Avoiding certain situations such as interviews, dates, public speaking	____ Reduce chance of disappointment/ rejection ____ Avoid anxiety and potential low mood if things don't go right Other:	____ Not reaching personal goals ____ Lack of opportunity to experience a sense of achievement Other:
____ Going only certain places or doing certain things with particular people	____ Decrease anxiety ____ Give greater sense of predictability Other:	____ Resentment ____ Overreliance on certain people ____ Restricted lifestyle Other:

____ Using alcohol/ drugs (prescribed, over the counter, or illegal/ recreational)	____ Increase feelings of self-confidence ____ Decrease anxiety ____ Improve mood ____ Give a buzz ____ Provide a sense of well-being Other:	____ Out-of-control behavior and regrets ____ Hangovers/ crashing ____ Negative impact on other areas of life ____ Addiction Other:
____ Perfectionism/ controlling self or others	____ Avoid criticism ____ Means of controlling anxiety Other:	____ Very hard to achieve and maintain Other:
____ Overpreparing	____ Increase the likelihood of success ____ Avoid disappointment ____ Decrease anxiety Other:	____ Time consuming ____ Hard work ____ In certain circumstances, increased likelihood of things being stilted and difficult ____ Exhaustion Other:

Coping Strategy	Intended Functions	Possible Unintended Consequences or Drawbacks
____ Internally and externally monitoring situations as they happen[1]	____ Help you respond quickly to a situation ____ Prevent negative things happening Other:	____ Hypervigilance putting you on edge ____ Increased likelihood of your noticing negative things ____ Keeps you from being in and enjoying the moment ____ Attention of others drawn to you due to your constant checking or appearance of being anxious Other:
____ Overthinking a situation before it happens and/ or going over it excessively after it has happened	____ Prepare yourself for situations ____ Prepare yourself for the possible consequences of situations Other:	____ Increased focus on threat and subsequent anxiety ____ Increased likelihood of predicting or finding problems Other:

---

1   Internal monitoring may mean you are constantly checking your heart rate, breathing, or the thoughts and images in your mind. External monitoring may involve constantly checking others to see if they are looking at you.

____ Overplanning situations, such as making sure where the toilet is, where the exit is	____ Provide quick escape route in the event of difficulties ____ Decrease anxiety Other:	____ Increased hypervigilance and anxiety in the long run Other:
____ Self-criticizing	____ Criticize self before someone else does ____ Keep yourself in check ____ Prepare yourself for difficult things that may happen Other:	____ Lowering of mood ____ Increasing anxiety Other:
____ Food fads and constant monitoring of food intake	____ Avoid rejection on the grounds of how you look ____ Focus on it, avoid dealing with other things ____ Feel sense of pride Other:	____ Eating problems, such as bulimia and anorexia Other:
____ Overeating	____ Sense of contentment or soothing while eating Other:	____ Guilt ____ Shame ____ Weight gain and the development of a negative body image Other:

Coping Strategy	Intended Functions	Possible Unintended Consequences or Drawbacks
____ Hurting oneself by cutting/burning	____ Sense of release ____ Punishment ____ Control emotions Other:	____ Injury ____ Scars ____ Shame Other:
____ Wearing makeup excessively	____ Cover up perceived deficits Other:	____ Difficult to maintain ____ May warn others off Other:
____ Constantly apologizing for things	____ Appease others ____ Decrease the likelihood that others will attack or reject you	____ Resentment of others ____ Others take advantage of you
____ Seeking reassurance from others	____ Reduce anxiety Other:	____ May increase anxiety in the long run as you become reliant on others ____ Others become frustrated with you, affecting your relationships Other:

Of course, we may all use these coping strategies from time to time. Problems occur when we use them to excess.

In addition to resulting in the specific unintended consequences or drawbacks outlined above, many of these strategies can cause more universal problems, such as putting strain on our close relationships. More importantly, they can also prevent us from building our self-confidence, because we tend to attribute any success to the strategies themselves and the failures to ourselves alone. This often reinforces our key concerns and fears, creating a vicious cycle. Sad and frustrating, isn't it?

PUTTING ALL THE ELEMENTS TOGETHER: A FORMULATION

The following case study is designed to illustrate how all of this information can be drawn together by means of a *formulation*. As with the other case studies in this book, Andy is not a real person but an amalgamation of the stories of several people. First a description of key elements in his life will be provided, followed by a formulation of these. After you read Andy's story, exercise 8 will help you develop a formulation based on your own experiences.

• *Andy's Story*

Andy was the youngest of three children. He was born with a congenital heart defect, which meant that he had to have surgery when he was very young and regular checkups until his early twenties. His parents were understandably concerned about his physical well-being and were overprotective of him.

At their insistence Andy did not take part in sports at primary school, just to be on the safe side, although he wished he could and felt left out and "different" as a consequence. At secondary school he could take part in certain sports but had to sit out of anything that was thought to be too strenuous, such as cross country, football, and sprinting. Secretly, Andy sometimes worried about his physical health but did not tell his family, as he didn't want to worry them or give them further reason to be overprotective.

His elder brother and sister seemed very confident. When as a little boy Andy needed to take the money from his piggy bank to the bank, his sister did it for him. While his brother was a keen football player, Andy was always on the sidelines.

At his all-boys school, Andy did well academically. Whenever he had homework, he received help from his brother, sister, or parents. It was after he left home for college and began mixing with lots of new people from diverse backgrounds that Andy started to have difficulties. Many of the people he knew from in his classes and dorm were active in sports. Although five years earlier Andy had received the all clear from his doctors, he'd had limited opportunity to develop athletically. Everyone his own age had always been so much better at sports than he was, and he'd chosen not to play with the younger boys, as he feared losing face with his peers. It had been easier to say he still had physical health problems, and this pattern continued.

Andy was homesick but felt stupid saying so to his family, his new set of friends, and his old ones. When he went out with friends, everyone else seemed to be talking about sports or about people he didn't know, and he felt excluded. In order to cope, Andy developed the habit of having a couple of drinks beforehand, as it seemed to help the flow of conversation. The downside (unintended consequence) was that a couple of hours later he would find that he was drunker than everyone else. His new friends ribbed him about this. Andy laughed along with them, even contributed to or initiated the derogatory comments, but secretly he was feeling more and more socially isolated.

Having had limited contact with girls before leaving home, Andy was very anxious around the opposite sex. He clammed up. Rather than risk looking stupid, he simply avoided speaking to girls and made out to his friends at home that he was seeing a girl at school and told his friends at school that he had a girlfriend back home.

Constantly finding excuses to go home, Andy spent increasing amounts of time there. His sister and brother had moved away, but Andy used his time there to do homework and catch up with friends who hadn't gone away to school. The problem was, he didn't really feel close to them now either. Sometimes he would

sit quietly and listen to them; other times he would try to impress
them with stories about events, friendships, and conquests, all of
which were fictitious.

After graduating, Andy went to work for his uncle in the
family business. This was great news; the pay was good, and
there was no need for endless job applications. As time went
on, however, he realized that some of his coworkers resented his
getting the job "because he was family." They seemed to think he
was spying for his uncle and therefore excluded him from their
conversations. Andy would worry they were talking about him
and would sit on his own in the cafeteria, pretending to read
a book or his texts. Soon he felt isolated once more. His mood
was generally low, and he avoided a range of anxiety-provoking
situations. He felt ashamed about the way he believed he had let
things get out of control and how he was dealing with things now,
and he increasingly chided himself: Pull yourself together. What's
wrong with you? You should be grateful for this job, your health,
and supportive family. You're pathetic.

Diagram 3 is a formulation of Andy's story. It's important to remember that no formulation will ever give a complete account of someone's life and circumstances, but this one should give an idea of how problems developed for Andy and how they were reinforced by subsequent events.

As you see, the first box has a range of different influences and experiences that span Andy's life to date. Some of the concerns, strategies, and unintended consequences appear to be a direct consequence of his life experiences, while others seem to be the result of things he has done to try to deal with certain problems. In addition, it could be argued that some of the unintended consequences could themselves be classed as experiences (and therefore be placed in the first box).

What's important in any formulation is to put the elements together in a way that makes sense to the person involved and to give a comprehensive account of how problems have developed and how they are maintained. Remember, the exercise that follows is for you alone and not something that is going to be scrutinized by others.

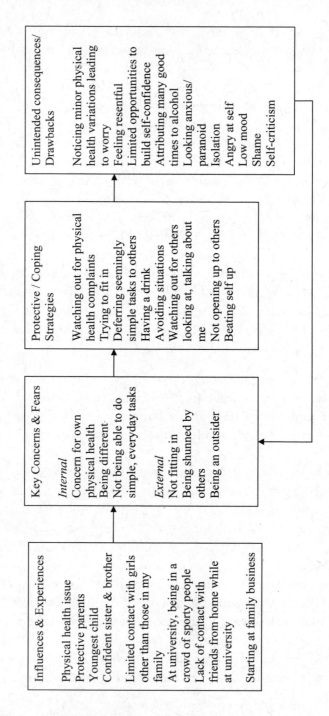

Influences & Experiences	Key Concerns & Fears	Protective / Coping Strategies	Unintended consequences/ Drawbacks
Physical health issue	*Internal*	Watching out for physical health complaints	Noticing minor physical health variations leading to worry
Protective parents	Concern for own physical health	Trying to fit in	Feeling resentful
Youngest child	Being different	Deferring seemingly simple tasks to others	Limited opportunities to build self-confidence
Confident sister & brother	Not being able to do simple, everyday tasks	Having a drink	Attributing many good times to alcohol
Limited contact with girls other than those in my family	*External*	Avoiding situations	Looking anxious/ paranoid
At university, being in a crowd of sporty people	Not fitting in	Watching out for others looking at, talking about me	Isolation
Lack of contact with friends from home while at university	Being shunned by others	Not opening up to others	Angry at self
Starting at family business	Being an outsider	Beating self up	Low mood
			Shame
			Self-criticism

Diagram 3: Andy's formulation

Exercise 8: Your Own Formulation

Using the information you collected in exercises 5, 6, and 7, use the blank diagram 4 to develop your own formulation. As you fill in the different boxes, it is likely that you will become aware of issues that you need to think about more. For example, you might have reflected earlier on a way of coping, but you may not have noted its potential drawbacks. Or you may have remembered an early life experience but not reflected on the key concerns or fears that were associated with it.

You may want to use your notebook or journal to experiment with different formulations, or alternative ways of putting together the information that you've collected. The additional space may allow you to play around with the content.

When you have completed this exercise, so you are satisfied that you have a good account of how your problems have developed and how you may be inadvertently maintaining them, it will be time to engage in the final exercise of this chapter.

Positive Changes in One Area Can Result in Positive Changes in Others

Although this book is aimed at building your self-confidence, it is likely that this exercise will highlight other areas of concern to you, such as anxieties, trauma, low mood, and shame. This is because the complexity of human psychology means that it is almost impossible to look at one area of our lives without reflecting on others. Although this may seem complicated, there are also benefits to it. More specifically, working on one area can often have a positive impact on many other parts of our psychological lives.

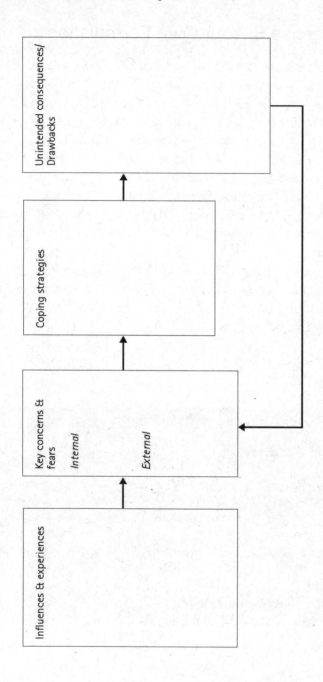

Diagram 4: Your own formulation of why problems have developed and how they are maintained

Later in the book, you will return to this exercise and review it from a different frame of mind. You will also use this exercise when you focus on compassionate letter writing.

Exercise 9: Making Sense of Things

Standing back from all the emotions generated by the previous exercises in this chapter, look at your formulation as a whole. Does it explain why you are in the situation you find yourself in right now? If the formulation did not apply to you but applied instead to someone you cared about, would it make sense then?

If the formulation does not make sense to you, either in how your difficulties have developed or in the way they are maintained, spend a little longer on it.

If you find that you are being self-critical or undermining yourself because of some aspect of the formulation, make a note of this so that you can come back to it later. This may become the focus of imagery work, compassionate letter writing, chair work, or compassionate alternative-thought worksheets.

CONCLUSIONS

We are who we are due to a combination of our biology (nature) and our experiences (nurture). At every point in life, we are attempting to do our best to get by or meet our needs in a difficult world and with a complex brain. Unfortunately, however, the things that we do to cope with situations can sometimes have drawbacks in terms of our well-being and self-confidence. Hindsight means that we may look back on situations and judge ourselves harshly, or think that we chose the easier rather than the more helpful option or else simply got things wrong. This may result in self-criticism and self-recrimination.

It is impossible to turn back time and recall all of the reasons we acted in certain ways at particular points. What is important now is that we attempt to understand ourselves compassionately, learn from experience, and nurture both ourselves and our self-confidence.

5

What Is Compassion?

Compassion is not religious business, it is human business,
it is not luxury, it is essential for our own peace and
stability, it is essential for human survival.

—Dalai Lama XIV

This chapter will look at how the compassionate-mind approach defines
compassion. It will examine the compassionate mind, or mindset, in
comparison and relation to different states of mind, such as those we
experience in the context of threatening or competitive situations.[1]
It will then discuss the attributes and skills of the compassionate
mindset. A better understanding of this will give you an idea of what
you are hoping to achieve and also of the skills needed to boost your
self-confidence.

---

1   Within the compassionate-mind approach, we refer to *mindsets*, which integrate
different mental components or capabilities, making up a "set."

TRADITIONAL VIEWS OF COMPASSION

Most of the early writings on compassion were conducted in the context of religious traditions. Compassion is referred to as a key part of such religions as Jainism, Islam, Buddhism, Judaism, Christianity, and Hinduism.

While views of compassion slightly differ among the major religions, and even between texts within the same tradition, compassion is almost universally accepted to mean, in everyday terms, a deep sympathy and sorrow in the face of suffering, be it our own or that of someone else, together with a motivation or commitment to alleviate distress.

Although the compassionate-mind approach acknowledges both secular and religious views, it also incorporates or updates our understanding with present-day research, which informs us of how the brain orients itself and operates within the context of compassion.

How Mindsets Work

You may have experience with *apps*, or applications, that turn your phone into a camera, a calculator, a gaming system, or an Internet connection. In such modes, your phone is still a phone, but with different applications running, the keys or areas of the screen behave differently. In turn, you behave differently with the phone, maybe holding it in a different way and viewing it from another angle.

A mindset could be thought of as an app for your "smart brain." In one mode you can be competitive, resulting in certain ways of thinking, different motivations, and even different postures. By contrast, engaging with a compassionate mindset will switch the competitive functions off and replace them with a range of different thoughts, motivations, and feelings.

THE COMPASSIONATE-MIND APPROACH TO COMPASSION

Research suggests that our brains possess a range of mindsets that work in the following ways:

- They orient our thinking and reasoning (including both verbal thoughts and images).

- They orient our attention.

- They recruit certain feelings.

- They motivate us in certain directions, resulting in particular behaviors.

Different mindsets turn on certain functions and capabilities in the brain while turning off others. Understanding that compassion is one of these mindsets is a key part of this chapter.

Compassion in Contrast to Other Mindsets

The following three exercises will give you the opportunity to experience and compare different mindsets.

Exercise 10: The Threat Mindset

Imagine, for a moment, you are in a room full of people, and you suddenly notice that someone is scrutinizing you. His eyes are narrow, and his facial expression suggests he is viewing you in a negative way. This is likely to trigger your *threat mindset*.

After thinking yourself into this mindset, spend a few minutes thoroughly exploring it by answering the following questions:

- What is your attention focused on?

- What are you thinking?

- What emotions do you feel?

- What sensations do you feel in your body?

Now think about what is likely to have been going on. Your attention will have been narrowed and focused on the threat and on yourself in relation to it. It is likely that your thoughts will have become fixed on what you think the apparently hostile person is thinking of you. You may start to wonder what is wrong with you, or you may tell yourself that they have noticed something you already feel uncomfortable about, maybe with respect to your appearance, your behavior, or you as a person. You may experience anxiety or maybe anger, and these feelings may be associated with a range of different physiological reactions, such as increased heart rate, changes in your breathing pattern, and degree of bodily tension. In addition, you may feel motivated to leave, to constantly check if the person is still looking, or to confront the person who is scrutinizing you.

Finally, take a few deep breaths and let the experience fade from your mind.

Exercise 11: The Competitive Mindset

Now, imagine you are running a marathon for which you have trained for months and months. You are approaching the final 1,000 meters, and it looks as though there is a possibility of beating your personal best or of even finishing before the rest of your training team. This situation is likely to trigger your *competitive mindset*. After thinking yourself into this mindset, spend a few minutes thoroughly exploring it by answering the following questions:

- What is your attention focused on?

- What are you thinking?

- What emotions do you feel?

- What bodily sensations do you feel?

Now think about what is likely to have happened. You were probably thinking *Come on, push yourself, beat your personal best*. Your mind would be full of images of crossing the line to the cheers of the spectators. If you were thinking about your fellow competitors at all, it is unlikely that you were wondering how they were doing. Instead, you would have been wondering if you could beat them, or your attention might have been fixed solely on yourself and getting to the finish line. As you approached it, you might have experienced a surge of exhilaration that helped you forget the blisters on your feet and the pain in your limbs. Suddenly, you seemed to have a boost of extra energy. You were motivated toward the finish line, and that was all that mattered to you.

Finally, take a few deep breaths and let the experience fade from your mind.

Exercise 12: The Compassionate Mindset

Imagine for a moment that you are visiting a friend or coworker for the first time since she suffered bereavement. On the way, you may initially wonder how the visit will go or whether you will be of any help to her, and you may feel a bit anxious about it. As your friend opens the door, you notice a look of profound sorrow, tears in her eyes. This situation is likely to trigger your *compassionate mindset*. After thinking yourself into this mindset, spend a few minutes thoroughly exploring it by answering the following questions:

- What is your attention focused on?

- What are you thinking?

- What emotions do you feel?

- What bodily sensations do you feel?

Now think about what is likely to have happened. As soon as you encountered the bereaved person, your thoughts would be directed toward this person and how she was feeling. Any thoughts of yourself and your own concerns about the visit would be set aside. You may feel physically drawn toward the other person or feel the need to make eye contact. You may experience a deep sense of sorrow and the need to be of help (in whatever way your friend seems to require at that moment). This may mean giving a hug, talking, or "taking her out of herself" by going for a drink and filling in your friend on what's been happening.

Once again, take a few deep breaths and let the experience fade from your mind.

Reflection on Exercises 10 through 12

As you can see from the scenarios described above, we all have the capacity for different mindsets that organize our brains in different ways. Some mindsets make us focus on ourselves, some on other people; some drive us toward certain things, some away from them.

In each of the scenarios outlined, we are still ourselves, but the ways in which our brains operate are different.

Mindsets and Self-Confidence

This book aims to help you develop self-confidence through a compassionate mindset. In chapter 1, you saw that while warmth and kindness are central to compassion, so too are strength and courage. A compassionate mindset will help you recognize when things are difficult and give you the strength and courage to do something about it instead of constantly undermining yourself and your efforts.

Exercise 13: Comparing Different Mindsets

This exercise illustrates further how different mindsets compare to each other and how the development of your compassionate mindset may stand you in good stead.

Consider Jim and Becky's story from chapter 1. As you will recall, Jim wanted to ask Becky out, but when he bumped into her, his self-confidence failed him. He ended up talking about something completely different. He found himself in a threat mindset.

Thinking about this situation, fill in the middle column of worksheet 4 with some ideas about Jim's mindset. Think about what thoughts Jim might have had, where his attention might have been, how he might have been feeling, and what he might have been motivated to do. It is important to remember that the exercise is asking you to think about what might have been happening with Jim while he was in the situation, not before or after it but when he actually bumped into Becky.

Now, in contrast, imagine in the crucial moment that Jim was able to be compassionate toward himself. In this mindset, he still experiences anxiety and is not impervious to life's setbacks and disappointments, but he feels reassured that he will be okay in whatever situations he faces and will recover from any knocks he takes. He is able to keep his anxiety in check so that his threat system is not allowed to run the show.

Now complete the second column of the worksheet with some ideas about Jim's compassionate mindset.

Worksheet 4: Threat vs. Compassionate Mindset

	Threat Mindset	Compassionate Mindset
What thoughts might have been running through Jim's mind?		
Where would Jim's attention be focused?		
What emotions would Jim be likely to experience?		
What feelings might Jim experience in his body?		
How might Jim hold himself? How would his posture be in this situation?		
What would Jim be motivated to do?		

As you can see from each of the exercises in this chapter, different mindsets can influence our thinking, attention, bodily sensations, motivation, behavior, and even posture, in startlingly different ways. The aim is not to rid yourself of anxiety altogether but rather to be able to keep it in check by developing a compassionate mindset through which you can learn to regulate your threat system and build your self-confidence.

You may have found exercise 13 difficult, as this chapter has yet to look closely at the different attributes of compassion and how they complement each other. If so, it may be helpful to return to this exercise after finishing this chapter.

How Mindsets and Associated Emotions Relate to Each Other

Our mindsets are each associated with a particular way of thinking and feeling, as well as motivations and behaviors. Thus, they recruit or switch on certain functions of the brain. Although mindsets can sometimes be associated with a mixture of different emotions, there are certain emotions that do not have the capacity to coexist with others. In other words, one negates the other. This occurs naturally, but human beings are also able to manipulate it to their advantage. For example, research has demonstrated that if we are induced into a state of relaxation, we cannot simultaneously feel anxious; one state counteracts the other.

It is through the intervention of the compassionate mindset that you will hopefully learn how to turn down or turn off the sometimes troublesome threat system.

COMPASSIONATE ATTRIBUTES

After decades of research, Paul Gilbert has distinguished six *attributes* (or qualities) of compassion that are all experienced in the context of emotional warmth. Warmth is important, as it turns something that could be a purely intellectual concept into something with much greater emotional resonance. The six attributes are distinct from each other, but they are also closely related and complementary. They are outlined next, along with brief views of how each may apply to your efforts to build your self-confidence.

Care for Well-Being

This attribute involves a commitment and motivation to truly care for the well-being of yourself and others.

Care for well-being may mean making a commitment to face something you feel anxious about because you know it is in your best interest to do so, even if it is something you are fearful of doing.

Sensitivity to Distress

Sensitivity to distress involves noticing when you or others are distressed or experiencing difficult emotions. It also involves being open to such things so that you notice them.

The fact that you are reading this book suggests that you have noticed you are experiencing some difficulty with self-confidence. However, it is important that this sensitivity be coupled with warmth so that hostile thoughts, such as *I've got to pull myself together/sort myself out*, turn into nurturing ones, such as *I'm having a difficult time and it would be helpful if I acknowledged this and took steps to help myself.*

Sympathy

Sympathy is the ability to be moved by your situation, or that of others, and connect with the pain being experienced.

Sympathy in relation to difficulties with your self-confidence may involve recognizing the following (with warmth): *This is hard, and it's understandable that I struggle in this way.*

Empathy

Empathy allows us to think about the nature of our minds and those of others. It allows us to see things from different perspectives and, in the context of our difficulties, think about what we, or someone else, may need.

In relation to your self-confidence, empathy may help you work out exactly what you need at a specific point in time. This, of course, is similar to "care for well-being."

Nonjudgment

Nonjudgment involves understanding that human beings are complex. It is about not condemning things that occur in our lives and in our minds or that occur in those of others. This is in contrast to being judgmental, which is often associated with shame and criticism of ourselves and others. Nonjudgment does not, however, mean being detached. Remember, all of these attributes are experienced within the context of warmth.

Hopefully, after reading the material outlined in chapters 1 through 3 and making sense of your experiences in chapter 4, you will now be able to view yourself as a human being who, like many others, struggles with certain things. Viewing yourself in this way helps reduce self-criticism and shame while also increasing nonjudgmental warmth in relation to the things that have happened to you and the situation you find yourself in right now.

Distress Tolerance

Distress tolerance involves feeling difficult emotions despite an urge to suppress them or push them away. Such emotions may include anxiety, sadness, anger, jealousy, or guilt. Although at times it may be important to keep our emotions in check, it is imperative that we do not do this all the time, as this is widely considered to lie at the root of many psychological difficulties.

In relation to your self-confidence, being able to tolerate distress involves acknowledging the emotions you feel and giving them space. It may involve resisting the urge to avoid a problem and lead you to "feel the fear and do it anyway."[2]

---

2   The title of a book by Susan Jeffers.

SKILLS OF THE COMPASSIONATE MINDSET

In addition to compassionate attributes, the compassionate-mind approach also distinguishes a number of *skills* (or things that you can learn to do) to help harness and maintain the compassionate mindset. These skills are closely related to each other:

Compassionate Understanding

Practicing compassionate understanding involves understanding the reasons we are as we are and the situations we subsequently find ourselves in. It involves being supportive of ourselves and others.

Compassionate Imagery

When we are anxious, it is very easy to generate frightening images in our minds, images from the past or from the predicted future. Maybe, in the moment, we experience self-critical images. Compassionate images are supportive, understanding, kind, and encouraging and can be used to help us.

Compassionate Attention

Compassionate attention allows us to recognize times when things went well—or maybe when things didn't, but the situation turned out okay anyway—and to learn from this. It also helps us focus on things in a way that helps balance any negatives we may perceive or experience.

Compassionate Motives

Compassionate motives direct you toward things that enable you to flourish in the long term, supporting your well-being. Compassionate motives can also be experienced in relation to others.

Compassionate Behavior

Compassionate actions emerge from compassionate motives and involve our behaving in a way that is beneficial for our own well-being or that of others.

Compassionate Emotions

Feelings of warmth, support, kindness, and a sense of connectedness are all compassionate emotions.

HOW COMPASSIONATE ATTRIBUTES AND SKILLS FIT TOGETHER

Imagine a six-legged stool. Each leg would represent one of the six attributes of compassion. Such a frame would provide a solid and strong base. Remove any of the legs, and the stool would still be stable but a little less so. Now imagine that the stool seat is made up of a tight six-way cane weave, each strand representing one of the compassionate skills. See diagram 5.

Diagram 5: The compassion stool

These attributes and skills are integral to building and maintaining compassion. The more of these compassionate attributes and skills you can develop and use, the more robust your compassionate mind will be. But, of course, if you struggle with certain attributes, you needn't worry, for the structure still has a considerable amount of strength. Proceed with what you can do, and maybe later on return to what you find difficult. The structure of the stool represents compassion, the platform upon which you will build self-confidence.

HOW TO GAIN COMPASSIONATE ATTRIBUTES AND SKILLS

Although you may have these attributes and use these skills in your relationships with other people, you may not often have them or use them on yourself. This is, of course, very common. As these skills and attributes are crucial to developing self-compassion and ultimately to building your self-confidence, they will become the focus of later chapters in this book.

CONCLUSIONS

Compassion is a mindset. As we engage with this mindset, we turn off certain mental capacities and abilities while turning on others. The same can be said for when you engage with threat or competitive mindsets. Six compassionate attributes and six skills form the firm foundation on which self-confidence is built.

6

Obstacles to the Development of Self-Compassion

How wonderful it is that nobody need wait a single moment before starting to improve the world.

—Anne Frank

Many of us have no problem with being compassionate to others, but accepting compassion from others and practicing self-compassion can be a different matter. This can ultimately interfere with building self-confidence.

The biggest obstacles preventing us from accepting compassion from others and exercising self-compassion are the views and thoughts we may hold about compassion and about ourselves.

Emotional and environmental obstacles can also be very powerful. For example, feelings of self-compassion may bring up difficult and seemingly surprising emotions and memories that can interfere with the work involved in building self-confidence. You may also find that people who are close to you resist changes you're attempting to make, maybe because they have gotten used to seeing you in a certain way.

This chapter will look at some of the obstacles to self-compassion and their potential origins. It will focus on why such obstacles also have an impact on the development of self-confidence. It will then look at some ways to negotiate these obstacles.

TEN THOUGHTS THAT INTERFERE WITH PRACTICING SELF-COMPASSION

You may have thoughts or views that get in the way of practicing self-compassion. Even if you are unaware of any personal resistance to developing self-compassion, you may find it helpful to read through the statements below and note any that resonate with you.

1. Self-compassion is about self-pity.

Pity for others is often viewed as synonymous with looking down from a position of superiority or feeling sorry for someone, and pity for the self is often dismissed as wallowing. For many, feeling pity means not acknowledging someone's innate strength and resilience; those who are pitied are defined solely by the situation they find themselves in rather than as whole people. If this is how you define pity, then you should know that self-compassion is absolutely not about self-pity. It is, however, important to recognize that different people and cultures view the concept of pity in different ways. For example, Michelangelo's *Pietà* is a work of art depicting the mother of Christ holding her dead son's body. When many Italians speak of the sculpture, they reflect that this is the depiction of ultimate love and compassion. Within Italian culture, the word *pietà* has no negative connotation.

2. Self-compassion is about being selfish or self-centered.

In fact, self-compassion often brings with it a greater capacity to help oneself and, in turn, others. Having become more self-compassionate, people often report having greater strength to deal with conflicts and to become better friends, parents, and colleagues. Lack of self-compassion, by contrast, means that we are more likely to become immobilized or consumed by our own difficulties and therefore less able to help others.

3. You don't deserve compassion.

Self-compassion can be blocked by the belief that we are not worthy or deserving of it. If you feel you don't deserve compassion, it is likely that you are judging yourself or your actions negatively and experiencing high levels of shame. As previously discussed, this can undermine the development of your self-confidence. If you identify with this, hopefully the work you did in chapter 4, developing an understanding of your journey and the situation you find yourself in now, will have helped you address this belief. Later you will use compassionate imagery to help you review your formulation from chapter 4. A sense of being undeserving can also become the focus of compassionate alternative-thought work-sheets and compassionate letter writing, which will be covered later in this book.

For now, however, it may be helpful to think of your own sense of being undeserving of compassion as a fear that is challenging but not overwhelming. Encourage yourself to take things one small step at a time. Ask yourself, *What aspect of compassion don't I deserve?* and start with the aspects of compassion that you feel you do deserve. Begin slowly. As you work on specific areas, you may find that self-compassion may be a good thing, without the drawbacks you predicted. In other words, you won't suddenly become a bad person, get found out by others, and be humiliated if you practice some aspects of self-compassion. And once the ball is rolling, you may find that you actually want to try out other aspects of self-compassion.

If feeling undeserving really is tripping you up, there are two further things you could try. First, you may want to ask someone else if he or she thinks you deserve compassion. You should ask someone you trust, such as a family member or a friend, or you may want to seek professional advice from a therapist; your doctor or health professional may be able to recommend someone.

4. Your needs are not as important as other people's.

You may put your personal needs (including the need for self-compassion) on the back burner. This is a classic trap many people fall into, but when we perpetually put the needs of others first, we can subsequently feel a sense of anger and resentment. We feel taken for granted; we may feel as though we are uncared for and may become exhausted. Although we all do this at times, it is important that this way of thinking does not become extreme and immobilizing. Compassion is about striking a balance between focusing on ourselves and on others.

If you still think that the needs of others are more important than your own, start practicing self-compassion for the sake of others. You can always revert back to your old ways if you find it doesn't help.

5. Self-compassion is about letting yourself off the hook.

Key to self-compassion is understanding what's happened and what we've done, as well as the things that are happening and which we are doing. With a more balanced perspective, hopefully we can move away from self-criticism and shame. However, being understanding of yourself does not mean relinquishing responsibility, excusing your own actions, or letting yourself off the hook. Where appropriate, self-compassion is about taking responsibility for the things we might have done or continue to do. It then involves committing ourselves to changing things for the better where we can. This will hopefully be beneficial to both ourselves and others, as Tom's story illustrates.

•   *Tom's Story*

Tom had found himself being sarcastic toward others and keeping them at arm's length. People had commented that he could be "difficult," and some members of his family were no longer in contact with him. Through Tom's work on developing self-compassion, he began to face his own role in the development of his current difficulties. Instead of being self-critical about it, he began to understand why he had acted in certain ways. His actions were, in fact, understandable given some of the difficulties he had faced. With a compassionate mindset, he was able to resolve conflicts, adjust his behavior, and repair his relationships.

Of course, sometimes we put ourselves on the hook because we feel we deserve it. This clearly overlaps with a feeling of being undeserving. If this applies to you, you may want to ask yourself, *What elements of compassion do I deserve?* and start from there.

6. Self-compassion is a weak or soft option.

Contrary to what many people believe, developing self-compassion is not a weak or soft option. It involves facing our difficulties and experiencing a range of emotions that are uncomfortable. It then requires the commitment to change ourselves, which requires courage and strength.

In the context of building your self-confidence, compassion may involve speaking up for yourself even though you feel an overwhelming urge to remain quiet. It may involve facing your fears and doing something while every part of your being may seem to be arguing against it. It may involve letting people see the true you. All of this takes strength and courage.

7. Compassion means letting your guard down and leaving yourself open to threat.

Thanks to the human brain's "better safe than sorry" default setting and perhaps some adverse life experiences, our threat system often ends up running the show. This isn't very efficient and, bottom line, it's uncomfortable to be on edge so much of the time.

Practicing self-compassion can actually make your threat system run more efficiently; it makes you wiser and helps you decide when you need to put your guard up and when you don't. For example, if you live in a hostile environment, self-compassion will help you protect yourself. However, in relatively safe environments, it will give you the strength to face difficult situations and build your self-confidence.

If you find this is an obstacle for you, you can continue to keep your guard up as much as you want. As time goes on, however, by practicing self-compassion you may find that you are better able to distinguish between when you need to protect yourself and when self-protectiveness would be a waste of effort.

8. Allowing yourself to experience positive feelings will set you up for a fall.

Sometimes people are wary of positive moods or feelings of calmness or relaxation. Such experiences are associated with a fear that they are setting themselves up for a fall or that something may come out of the blue and they will be unprepared. Alternatively, some people believe that feeling good will attract negative things or payback. This is illustrated by Peter's story.

• *Peter's Story*

Peter had suffered a number of setbacks in his life, such as losing his job and having his first girlfriend split up with him. These events seemed to arrive out of the blue, so he started to be wary of bad things happening again. Of course, it was difficult for Peter to know whether being watchful would have prevented his job loss or the breakup. But it was certainly true that his strategy of constantly watching over his shoulder was now interfering with his life and was doing him no good. His hypervigilance had even been cited by a subsequent girlfriend as the reason she broke off their relationship. On balance, he wished he could return to the old carefree days.

Self-compassion can actually be the best way of preparing yourself for the difficulties and setbacks that life inevitably brings. This is because it builds your ability to cope with hard situations, and it's through coping with setbacks that self-confidence in our ability to cope increases. If fear of falling gets in the way of your experiencing positive feelings, it may be helpful just to think, *I'll give it a go. I can always revert to my old ways.*

Obviously, this section of the book is focusing on views and thoughts that may form obstacles to acquiring self-compassion. Later this chapter will look at how certain emotions can become paired with each other in the brain, which can lead to the experience of difficult emotions swiftly succeeding pleasurable ones.

9. Self-compassion means not facing up to difficult emotions.

This is one of the most common misunderstandings relating to self-compassion. In fact, self-compassion is about facing up to and experiencing difficult emotions rather than turning away from them. Such emotions include sadness, anxiety, and anger. Self-compassion is about owning and validating such emotions and allowing ourselves to work through them instead of bottling them up (with adverse consequences for our mental well-being).

Self-compassion can help you develop the strength and courage to put yourself in anxiety-provoking situations so that you can build your self-confidence. If you wait until you feel confident enough to do something, you may be waiting a long time. Often we need to act first to start feeling self-confident.

10. It will be too hard or too overwhelming.

For some people, the thought of experiencing compassion, whether from others or from themselves, can evoke fear. Emotions that have been bottled up may surface with a destabilizing effect. Learning to practice self-compassion can be difficult, but suppressing emotions is thought to underpin many psychological difficulties. Working on them with self-compassion instead, though difficult in the short term, can ultimately be extremely rewarding.

Here are some strategies that can help:

- Go at a pace that is comfortable for you.

- Start gradually. Remember, if you were learning to swim, you would enter at the shallow end. Approach your work with self-compassion in a similar way.

- Engage in the work at a time when you feel you have the resources and support to do it.

- Combine this work with pleasurable activities, such as spending time with good friends, taking some time for yourself, going for walks, or engaging in other fun and healthy experiences.

- Time this work for when your life is relatively stable and free of stress.

- If you feel that you need the support of a professional, speak to your doctor or health practitioner about getting some form of psychological therapy.

EMOTIONAL OBSTACLES TO EXPERIENCING SELF-COMPASSION

Sometimes while attempting to build self-confidence, people are surprised to find difficult emotions and memories surfacing, and it can be extremely confusing.

• *Elaine's Story*

Elaine had found the mindfulness components of our therapeutic work together really helpful, but she felt overwhelming anxiety, tinged with anger, when we moved on to engaging with exercises aimed at evoking self-compassion. She had experienced similar emotions when she disclosed difficult issues during the early days of therapy, but she had explained it away to herself as part of getting to know her therapist. In fact, those feelings were an early indication of what she would experience later on.

To make sense of these emotions, we reviewed Elaine's early life experiences, and she disclosed that her parents had been unpredictable in their responses to her at key times in her life. Sometimes they were comforting, but other times they were dismissive or even punishing. Elaine recalled a number of significant memories. For example, one day she had fallen from her bike and run screaming to her stepmother. Instead of the comfort she had sought, her screams were met with anger. Although Elaine said that she thought she had already "dealt with these things," such events made sense of why self-compassion continued to evoke difficult emotions for her. Understanding this was a key element in our work together. Noticing and accepting such emotions, talking about and allowing herself to feel them, were pivotal to Elaine becoming more self-compassionate.

The psychological concept of conditioning, as well as neuroscience research, accounts for why some individuals have emotions that seemingly become paired with others. The phrase "neurons that fire together wire together" encapsulates this very simply. In basic terms, if we are punished for feeling anger as a child, it is likely that anger will become paired with anxiety (the anxiety we feel before, during, or after the punishment) in adult life. Anger may occur simultaneously with anxiety or seemingly be replaced by it (in other words, situations that are likely to produce anger produce anxiety instead). In a second example, if a child goes to her parent when she's upset and, instead of receiving a hug, she is repeatedly ignored, rejected, or even humiliated, that child will begin to link the experience of needing closeness with the experience of anger, anxiety, or sadness. While young, this child may learn to avoid approaching her parent, but as an adult, she may experience confusing emotions whenever she feels a sense of closeness to someone else.

These strong and seemingly contradictory emotions can also be paired with vivid memories. Sometimes the emotion comes first, sometimes the memory, and at other times we experience them simultaneously. Although some individuals find that such memories are useful to them, as they help account for why they are feeling certain emotions, other people find them extremely difficult to handle. Deborah Lee has written *The Compassionate Mind Approach to Recovering from Trauma*, which focuses on emotional memories relating to traumatic experiences. If you have difficulty handling feelings associated with certain memories, her book may be helpful to you (see resources).

Again, emotions can become linked, or wired, together. They can also be paired with difficult memories that burst into our minds uninvited. The feeling of compassion may subsequently evoke fear, anxiety, sadness, and anger. Understanding this can be the first step to dealing with it. You can then endeavor to work through your emotions and hopefully use compassion to soothe the difficult feelings.

Of course, if you find that this is too difficult to do on your own, then there is no shame in seeking the help or advice of others. Your doctor or health practitioner may be a good starting point to direct you to further help.

ENVIRONMENTAL OBSTACLES TO BUILDING SELF-CONFIDENCE

Many people who are attempting to build their own self-compassion and self-confidence find others around them resisting the significant changes they are attempting to make. The next three stories illustrate this problem.

•   *Henry's Story*

Henry developed the strength and motivation to start putting himself forward at work and doing things he would never have dreamed of attempting in the past. When he first volunteered to chair a work meeting, everyone in his department turned around in shock and looked at him. Two people even snickered while another said in a patronizing tone, "Are you sure?" This made Henry more anxious than ever. At the meeting the following week, more people than usual turned up. At difficult points, he noticed people rolling their eyes or once again snickering, as if they were just watching and waiting for him to mess up. He found people talked over him as he was speaking, which they didn't seem to do with more confident members of the team, and they were more likely to carry on conversations when he asked for certain discussions to come to an end.

• *Emma's Story*

Emma found that her sister and brother seemed to block her attempts to build her self-confidence. When she eventually plucked up the courage to get across her point about the care of their parents, they seemed to ignore what she was saying, quickly returning to their own discussion. In the past, Emma had always reluctantly gone along with their suggestions, fearful of how they would respond to her putting a different opinion forward. Now, as she attempted to make her point, she was overruled by them. It was almost as if she had to overassert herself to get anywhere. Simply stating her own point of view was getting her nowhere.

• *Patricia's Story*

After a pattern of never saying yes to nights out with work colleagues, Patricia decided that this was something she would like to change. Just getting an invitation, however, proved to be difficult. Eventually she had to invite herself. Then, as she was making plans for getting to and from the venue, she found that everyone else had already arranged shared taxis and lifts, based on previous nights out. She lived the farthest away and consequently had to plan to leave the venue early so she could get the last train home. All in all, she felt unwelcome and as if she were viewed as an inconvenience by everybody else.

The situations in which Henry, Emma, and Patricia found themselves were extremely difficult. It was almost as if, to receive an appropriate response, they had to work even harder than everyone else.

If you identify with these stories, some exercises later in this book may help you negotiate such environmental obstacles to building your self-confidence.

Of course, at times being more self-compassionate means thinking about whether we really need to change our environment. Do we want certain people in our lives, such as those who make us feel bad and refuse to change the way they behave around us, despite our best efforts to alter the situation? Self-compassion can help us with this, as it gives us the courage to face up to things but also, when necessary, to walk away from them.

Again, most people would want a compassionate teacher rather than a disciplinarian for their child—a teacher who nurtures the child's development, looks at difficulties and mistakes as opportunities to learn and grow, and is open and warm. It is interesting that intuitively we know what will help others but often find that our own inner teacher is hostile and critical: a carping voice that tells us we are stupid, pathetic, a waste of space, and unable to do certain things in certain areas of life. This can result in our simply shutting down, avoiding situations, or putting on a brave face. But if we can learn to adopt a more self-compassionate approach to our difficulties, we can build our self-confidence step-by-step. We can nurture ourselves into a state of well-being that will provide us with the resilience we need to take life's setbacks as they come and then move forward again.

If you have identified with any of the obstacles outlined in this chapter, the following section may be helpful. If not, you may want to skip ahead to the next chapter.

NEGOTIATING THE OBSTACLES TO SELF-COMPASSION

Self-compassion is not about letting yourself off the hook, venting emotions, and setting yourself up for a fall. Instead, adopting a self-compassionate mindset involves employing strength and courage to face difficult things, as well as tolerating and being sensitive to your own distress and that of others. The exercises in this section will provide you the means to objectively negotiate any obstacles you face.

Identifying the Obstacles

The first step is to identify any obstacles that are holding you back. For example, Patricia identified two areas of concern:

1. Accepting compassion from others: "I fear this would leave me open to upset and disappointment later. It is easier to disregard compassion from others, thinking *People are only saying that* and *If they really knew me, they wouldn't feel that way.*"

2. Developing self-compassion: "This would ultimately mean dropping my guard and would result in my not being prepared for things that happen in the future."

Despite her concerns, Patricia was also worried that if she did not do anything, she would continue to be "walked all over" by others and never be able to achieve the things she wanted to achieve within her work and personal life.

Having identified her personal obstacles, Patricia then looked at the pros and cons of both accepting compassion from others and developing self-compassion. She did this by completing the following worksheet.

Patricia's Worksheet: Pros and Cons of Accepting Compassion from Others and Developing Self-Compassion

Cons of Accepting Compassion from Others	Pros of Accepting Compassion from Others
I may be disappointed by people later. *I won't be as ready for being let down.*	*It may be a nice thing to do.* *It may help me challenge some of my own undermining.* *It may mean that I begin to feel more self-confident if I feel the support of others around me.* *I may get a warm glow.*
Cons of Developing Self-Compassion	**Pros of Developing Self-Compassion**
I may drop my guard and be less able to spot problems.	*Life may be easier.* *I may not be walked over as much, as I may feel stronger.* *It may help me achieve what I want to achieve, because life may be less stressful.* *It may stop me from undermining myself.* *It may develop my self-confidence.*

Patricia saw that, on balance, it would be worthwhile to work on developing her compassionate mind as a means of building her self-confidence.

Moving forward, she looked at each of her potential obstacles and began to address her concerns about accepting compassion from others and developing self-compassion. The following is Patricia's completed problem-solving worksheet, which lists what she could tell herself and what she could do differently.

Patricia's Completed Problem-Solving Worksheet

1. *If I become disappointed later, I can use self-compassion to help me with this.*

2. *If I am let down, I can remind myself that I have been let down before and come through it. This time will hopefully be different, though, as I am addressing the habit of self-criticism. I may also be able to go to other people who haven't let me down for their support.*

3. *I have learned that compassion isn't about dropping your guard but about helping it work more efficiently. I am not leaving myself unprotected.*

4. *I can always revert to my old ways if I need to.*

This closer examination of compassion and self-compassion ultimately resulted in Patricia deciding to give it a go. Although still a little skeptical, she decided it might be useful to try something new, if only so that she could say she had done it.

Exploring Your Obstacles

The following series of exercises will help you begin to identify and address your own obstacles to experiencing compassion from others and practicing self-compassion.

Exercise 14: Your Obstacles to Experiencing Compassion from Others

List any thoughts or feelings that restrict or prevent you from experiencing compassion from others. It may help to review the common obstacles discussed earlier in this chapter.

_____

_____

_____

_____

_____

_____

Exercise 15: Your Obstacles to Developing Self-Compassion

List any thoughts or feelings that restrict or prevent you from developing self-compassion. Again, it may help to review the common obstacles discussed earlier in this chapter.

_____

_____

_____

_____

_____

_____

Exercise 16: Pros and Cons of Accepting Compassion from Others

Use the following worksheet to explore the pros and cons of accepting compassion from others. List anything you can say to yourself or do differently that will help you address the cons and accept compassion from others.

Worksheet 5: Accepting Compassion from Others

Pros	Cons	Things you can say to yourself or do to help you address the cons

Exercise 17: Pros and Cons of Developing Self-Compassion

Use the following worksheet to explore the pros and cons of developing self-compassion. List anything you can say to yourself or do differently that will help you address the cons and develop self-compassion.

Worksheet 6: Developing Self-Compassion

Pros	Cons	Things you can say to yourself or do to help you address the cons

Exercise 18: Addressing Your Concerns

Returning to the last two worksheets, spend a little time reflecting on what measures you can take to help you cope with the obstacles you face in accepting compassion from others or in developing self-compassion. These measures may involve reassuring yourself or modifying your behavior as issues arise.

CONCLUSIONS

Obstacles to self-compassion are common. They can come in the form of the views and thoughts that we have developed over time in response to our environment, from emotional obstacles, and from pressure from those around us to remain the same. Some are relatively easy to overcome, others less so. If the ground covered in this chapter helps you move toward practicing self-compassion, this is good news.

A number of exercises later in this book may help you further in negotiating any obstacles in your path. You may find it helpful to return to this chapter after you've read the rest of the book and developed new skills.

7

Preparing for Compassion Using Mindfulness

Do not dwell in the past, do not dream of the future,
concentrate the mind on the present moment.

—Buddha

This chapter marks the beginning of the second part of this book, in which you will engage in a range of practical exercises meant to help build self-confidence by the application of self-compassion. Some exercises you will find useful, others perhaps less so. Once you have found exercises that suit you, you can begin to engage in them regularly as self-practice.

You can use the personal practice summary sheet (see end of preface) to note your ongoing thoughts on the exercises as you try them. You can then refer to these notes in the final chapter as you are putting together your personal plan for future self-practice.

Hopefully, you will approach these exercises with a spirit of curiosity as if you were trying a new food or hobby. The important thing is to remain open-minded and not let preconceptions prevent you from experimenting. Of course, this is not to suggest that you should continue to do something you don't like or that you find distasteful, but it is important to try it out.

MINDFULNESS

Evolution has provided human beings with the amazing ability to think about the past, present, and future. This has been hugely important for our survival. Unfortunately, however, this ability also means that we can find ourselves dwelling on past situations and predicting catastrophes in the future. This can activate our threat system and prevent our self-confidence from developing.

So how do we give our minds a break and stop getting caught up in the seemingly never-ending drama that goes on inside our heads? One approach that many people have found helpful originated in the Eastern religious traditions: mindfulness. More recently, mindfulness has been developed in the West as a practice to promote well-being. Practicing mindfulness has helped a wide range of people, from those who consider themselves to be psychologically well to those who identify themselves as suffering from anxiety and depression, among other difficulties.

The practice of mindfulness involves bringing your complete attention and calm awareness to the present moment—an awareness containing curiosity and nonjudgment. This may involve paying attention to things going on around you or to the thoughts occurring in your mind. The practice aims to help you:

- Slow things down

- Be in the present moment (instead of everywhere but)

- Become more observant about what is going on in your mind

- Make and implement choices about what you pay attention to, instead of letting your threat or drive system run the show

- Ultimately help you feel better and make better choices about whether to act on thoughts and feelings

Within the practice, as you become mindful that your attention has wandered from the moment, the key is to notice where your mind has moved to and without judgment but with curiosity bring the mind and attention back into focus.

The Mind's Tendency to Wander

Our minds wander all the time, and this is perfectly normal. Sometimes they are drawn to sounds, feelings, sensations, thoughts of what we are going to have for lunch, or what we watched on TV last night. They will be particularly drawn to things that are "on our mind." This may be something we need to do, something that has already been done, something we are looking forward to, or something we need to prepare for. The art of mindfulness means, in that moment when you realize that your mind has wandered, gently bringing your attention back to what you wish to focus on. You may find yourself making a whole list of things to do before realizing that you have moved your focus, but when you realize what is happening, you can gently adjust and bring your focus back to the practice.

Hopefully, this new skill will be helpful to you and will act as the foundation for a whole range of exercises to be introduced later that are aimed at helping you build your compassionate mind. In turn, you can then use your compassionate mind to build your self-confidence.

Mindfulness Can Be Both Difficult and Easy

Some people find it difficult because they fall into the trap of striving "to get it right"; their drive or threat system kicks in and takes over. Others may become panicky when they try these exercises, and if this is the case for you, some ideas offered later may help with this. For all of us, the busyness of our brains and the complexity of our lives mean that there can be built-in obstacles to mindfulness practice. That said, this could also be the most compelling reason to adopt it. On the positive side, mindfulness is something that you can easily practice. You need no special equipment to practice it; you need only time and motivation. It can be practiced while going for a walk, sitting quietly, in a busy place, or even washing your hands.

This chapter will cover a number of different exercises. If you can, try each one a number of times over a period of a week or so, and see also if you can increase the length of time you spend engaging in each exercise.

When I am talking people through these exercises, I aim to do so in a relaxed and soothing manner. The tone of my voice is soft and my speech is a lot slower than usual. I have tried to convey this in writing with lots of full stops to convey pauses and slowing down. As there is no way to convey a tone of voice here, I will merely suggest that, as you talk yourself through these exercises (be it out loud or with your inner voice), do so in a tone of gentleness and curiosity.

Hopefully, you will return to and use certain of these exercises later, and for this reason each one is written out in full.

Exercise 19: Mindfulness of Sound

Start by finding a location that is, as far as possible, free from major distractions. This place could be somewhere in your home, your garden, a park, or any other place you think may be suitable. It is a good idea to make yourself comfortable. This may mean sitting on a chair or bench, on the ground, or maybe on a sofa or bed.

Allow ten to fifteen minutes for this, as you may find the exercise helpful and soothing and wish to stay with it for some time.[1]

Ideally, you will sit in an upright posture, with your feet on the floor approximately hip-distance apart, your hands gently resting in your lap. You will feel a strength in your spine, yet a relaxation in your body and a sense of openness. If this position is difficult or feels uncomfortable, or if you would just prefer to do the exercise with legs crossed or while lying down, that's okay. The most important thing is to feel comfortable with your body and its position so you can immerse yourself in the exercise as fully as possible.

It is helpful if you can close your eyes for this exercise, knowing that at any time you can open them if you wish. Others may prefer to settle their gaze on a fixed point on the floor or somewhere low down.

Begin by noticing the sounds that are around you...maybe the song of a bird...the babble of water...the sound of the wind in the trees...maybe the hum of a computer...cars driving by...the banging of pipes...the rumble of your belly.

Notice the sounds getting louder or quieter...notice them coming and going...notice them with curiosity and without judgment.

When there are no sounds, observe the silence...let it be...without the hope for sound...just mindful until a sound comes.

When inevitably your mind wanders, notice with curiosity that it has wandered and where it has wandered. Then, without judgment, bring your attention back to the exercise.

When you are ready, gently bring your awareness back to your surroundings, look around you, and maybe stretch.

---

1   With any of these exercises, the suggested times are merely guidelines. If you prefer to engage in the exercises for a much longer or shorter time, this is absolutely fine.

Reflection on Exercise 19

It is highly likely that your mind will have wandered from time to time during this exercise. It may have wandered to things that are going on in your life, things that have happened, or things that are likely to happen. Your mind may have wandered to what you heard people saying, questioning whose car door was banging, where a hum was coming from, or why your stomach was rumbling. This is perfectly normal. The trick isn't to keep your mind from wandering, but, when you notice it has, to bring your attention back to the task without judgment.

You may have noticed things slowing down during this exercise and feeling more relaxed. Although there is increasing evidence that mindfulness can be helpful to those suffering from sleep problems, the purpose of this particular exercise is not to fall asleep but to create a sense of calm awareness in the present moment and provide a space into which you can build self-compassion. This, in turn, will help build your self-confidence. It is for this reason that I recommend your doing this exercise in a sitting position rather than lying down.

After completing each of the mindfulness exercises in this chapter, it may be helpful to write down some reflections in your notebook or on your personal practice sheet. In addition, if your mind wandered to particular things during the exercise, it may also help to make a note of this. These reflections may provide useful information for future exercises.

Exercise 20: Mindfulness of Bodily Sensations

Start by finding a location that is, as far as possible, free from major distractions. Choose a place where you feel comfortable and can be for ten to fifteen minutes. If possible, sit in an upright posture, with strength in your spine and a sense of openness in your body. It is helpful if you can close your eyes for this exercise, or you may prefer to settle your gaze on a low fixed point.

Notice the sensations in your own body...notice your breath slowly moving in and out...in and out...notice the rise and fall of your chest or your belly...notice the sensations your breath brings with it...notice your rib cage expanding then contracting...notice the temperature of your body... the warmth in your chest...notice how your body feels supported...move your attention around your body, from place to place, and notice how it feels.

When your mind wanders, which it will, gently and curiously notice where it has wandered and, without judgment, bring your attention back to the exercise.

Sometimes your body will feel tense; you may feel some pain or discomfort. If this is the case, just notice the tension, pain, or discomfort and then move your attention to another part of your body.

When you are ready, gently bring the exercise to an end and become more aware of your physical environment.

Reflection on Exercise 20

Because this exercise focuses on the body, you may have noticed areas of tension, pain, or discomfort. Mindfulness is increasingly found to be a helpful practice for those experiencing pain. If you notice tension, pain, or discomfort, be mindful of it, without the need to do anything about it, and then gently and without judgment bring your attention back to the exercise.

For some, concentrating on their breathing or body can be difficult. It may increase anxiety or uncomfortable physical sensations. Some people find that these sensations decline as they continue to practice. However, if this remains difficult for you, do not spend too long on this exercise. As you can see, there are many other mindfulness exercises to try.

Things That May Assist You in Your Practice

During these exercises, you are encouraged to close your eyes or lower your gaze. Obviously this makes reading difficult. It may help to make your own recording of the instructions, using a calm, quiet voice. Alternatively, sound files can be found on the Compassionate Mind Foundation website (www.compassionatemind.co.uk). As you become more familiar with the exercises, it is likely that you will be able to practice them from memory.

Exercise 21: Mindfulness of Breathing

If you found focusing on your body or the sensation of breathing particularly difficult in exercise 20, it is likely that you will find this exercise problematic too. However, many people find focusing on their breathing particularly helpful as a mindfulness practice. This exercise is often associated with a slowing down of your breathing to a comfortable and regular rate. For some, it involves noticing how the breath affects one part of the body, such as the belly, the nose, or the chest; for others, it involves focusing somewhere else or on a combination of these things.

If possible, do this exercise sitting with a feeling of strength and openness. This is to counteract any tendency you may experience to become so relaxed that you fall asleep.

Start by finding a place that is, as far as possible, free from major distractions, somewhere you can be for ten to fifteen minutes. It is helpful if you can close your eyes for this exercise, but you may prefer to settle your gaze on a low fixed point.

Sit quietly for a moment and bring your attention to your breathing. Be aware of your breath coming into your body...slowly and evenly...maybe you notice the sensation of air coming into and leaving your nose...maybe the rise and fall of your belly...maybe you are aware of your breath in your chest, rising and falling, or your rib cage expanding then contracting...move your awareness around your body and, wherever it is most

comfortable to notice your breathing, bring your awareness to that area...
now just settle and experience your breathing...in and out.

When you are ready, gently bring the exercise to an end and become
more aware of your physical environment.

Our Fast-Paced Lives Have an Impact on Us

It is worth reflecting on the ways that modern life has decreased the
opportunities, as well as the motivation, for being lost or absorbed in
an activity or moment, without a sense of urgency or need to think
about other things. We now live fast-paced lives, and many activities
that we used to engage in mindfully are either no longer valued or
needed.

For example, in days gone by, our parents and their parents would
absorb themselves in the task of making bread. They would hand-
wash clothes, tend the land, darn socks, and repair shirts. This is not
to say that they never did these things with any sense of urgency,
worry, or upsetting thoughts, but there were simply more opportunities
to focus completely on the activity at hand.

Now the pressures of life mean that if I am waiting to see the
dentist, I am likely to be checking my email; when I peel the vegeta-
bles, I may also be watching the TV or making a phone call. If I don't
practice mindfulness, it is easy to let a whole day go by when I have
not consciously focused my mind just on the moment.

Whether the object or focus of the mindfulness practice is
walking, breathing, washing my hands, or drinking coffee, mindfulness
allows me and many others to appreciate the moment and s...l...o...w
...d...o...w...n.

Reflection on Exercise 21

If you found either this exercise or the bodily sensations exercise
difficult, it may be helpful to engage in one of the anchoring practices
(exercises 22 or 23) alongside it. Alternatively, you may find it helpful
to gently repeat in your mind the statement *slowing down* as you engage
with this exercise, so you can take some of the intensity away. You may
also want to do this exercise with another activity, such as walking.

Exercise 22: Mindfulness of a Visual Anchor Point

Anchor points can be really helpful in mindfulness practice. Visual anchor points are something stationary on which you choose to fix your gaze. It usually helps to choose an anchor point a few feet away and on the floor or low down so that your eyes will be partially closed and less aware of visual distractions.

Your anchor point can be something that you notice in your environment, such as a chair leg, a plant, a piece of curbstone, or a pattern in the flooring. Alternatively, it could be something you always use and take with you, such as a ball, a stone, a bag, or a book.

Once again, start by finding a place that is, as far as possible, free from major distractions, somewhere you can be for ten to fifteen minutes. Adjust your posture as you have done previously.

Now identify a fixed anchor point on which you can hold your gaze. It may be something already there or something you place on the ground.

Now observe your anchor point: observe its shape, its edges… observe its color and texture…observe how at times it may be in sharp focus, at others it may become fuzzy in places…just observe the object.

When you are ready, gently bring your awareness back to your surroundings and look around you.

Reflection on Exercise 22

During mindfulness exercises, your attention might wander to any number of things, but while your eyes are open, there will be many sources of distraction. Sometimes these are moving things, such as a leaf fluttering by, a person passing, or a bird in flight, but often they are tricks our minds and sight play on us. For example, we may suddenly see a shadow when nothing is moving, or we may experience double vision. As with anything that takes our attention away from the exercise, this is perfectly normal. Once again the trick is to be mindful that your attention has wandered and bring it back to the practice.

If you are uncomfortable or apprehensive about doing exercises with your eyes closed, this is a good exercise to do in preparation for them. Alternatively, it can be used as a starting point for future exercises. People often find that they feel more confident about closing their eyes if they know they can open them at any time to see a visual anchor point.

Exercise 23: Mindfulness of a Tactile Anchor Point

In this exercise, instead of using a visual anchor point, you will use a tactile one. This may be something like a stone, a key ring, a piece of jewelry, or a purse or wallet. It should be something you can easily hold in one or two hands. It is also important to pick something that isn't associated with difficult emotions that could interfere with the exercise.

Once again, start by finding a place that is, as far as possible, free from major distractions, somewhere you can be for ten to fifteen minutes.

Now just hold the object in your hand or hands and notice how it feels...experience its weight...notice the texture of the item...maybe it's soft, maybe it's hard...maybe it's a combination of the two...notice the temperature of the object and how it feels when you manipulate it in your hands...feel how it is against your skin...continue with the exercise and when your mind wanders, notice with curiosity where it has wandered to and, without judgment, bring it back to the exercise.

When you are ready, gently bring the exercise to an end and become more aware of your physical environment.

Reflection on Exercise 23

Some people pick a different and novel object each time they do this exercise. Others find that it is more helpful to do this practice with the same object each time. The importance lies not in what you choose to use but whether the object is helpful to you in your practice.

Again, you may want to use this exercise in conjunction with some of the earlier exercises; it can provide you with an anchor point, if needed, when your eyes are closed.

Exercise 24: Mindful Walking

For some people, sitting and engaging in mindfulness exercises can prove difficult due to pain; others may not be able to find the time to sit still for an exercise or may not see it as a good use of time. Of course, if you find yourself in the latter two categories, I would encourage you to make time, so you can see for yourself that these exercises are actually extremely helpful in all manner of ways.

If, however, sitting is difficult for you—or you need further persuasion on the benefits these exercises—I would ask you to engage in mindful walking. Alternatively, you may simply prefer this form of mindfulness or to use it as a helpful addition to your practice.

During this exercise, you can either focus on one specific element of your experience, such as the sensation of walking or the things you can see, or you can slowly switch your attention between different things, working through the senses—from physical sensations on your skin, to sounds, to things you can see, and maybe to your breathing. Play around with the exercise and find the format that is most helpful to you.

Find somewhere to walk that will be, as far as possible, free from distractions. A busy street may not be the best place to start. Similarly, a local park, at a time when you are likely to see lots of people you know, may prove distracting.

Stand for a moment and feel the ground beneath your feet...feel the strength in your legs supporting you...now, as you find yourself walking, become aware of what the air feels like on your skin, maybe hot, maybe cold...maybe you can feel the warmth of the sun, droplets of rain or the breeze on your face...notice the sounds as they come and go...let curiosity rather than judgment fill your mind...notice nature around you, the plants, the trees, or look into the sky and see the clouds above or the pattern of the open sky...notice smells as they come and go...experience how it feels to walk on the ground.

When you feel ready, gently bring the exercise to an end and become more aware of your physical environment.

Reflection on Exercise 24

Mindful walking does not mean walking to get somewhere but walking to be mindful. That said, the exercise can easily be tied into everyday life, and for this reason many people find that it becomes a component of their self-practice. You may regularly have to walk a certain route to get somewhere; you may walk your dog or like to engage in physical exercise. If you are tying the exercise into a walk that you need to do, make sure that you allow yourself extra time so your mind isn't bombarded with associated thoughts.

You may have noticed that the other exercises focus on one sense, whereas this one focuses on a range of different things, such as the experience of the ground underfoot, the sensation of the air, the sounds around you. For some people, the wider focus proves helpful; for others, it is more helpful to attend to one thing at a time. This is a purely personal choice.

Once again, your mind will wander, especially because you have your eyes open. Your mind may wander even more so if you have a particular destination. Whenever you become mindful that your attention has wandered, notice where it has gone and gently bring it back.

How Mindfulness Can Help with Overstriving

Chapter 3 introduced the concepts of *value achievers* and *need achievers*, plus *growth seekers* and *validation seekers*. People who lack self-confidence can often become so caught up in striving to please others to gain recognition and approval that they can forget to experience pleasure in the moment. If you recognize this in yourself, over the next week, it may help simply to be mindful of the *process* of working toward a goal versus *achieving* the goal. Take a breath and bring your complete attention to the moment. If doing this is helpful, you may want to incorporate it into your daily practice. If you find doing this difficult, it could become the focus of later work. Chapter 13 will explore the practice of savoring positive experiences, which involves appreciating the moment, and this may help with your mindfulness practice.

As you are mindfully walking, there's a good chance of things being totally disrupted by bumping into someone you know, someone asking you for directions, or by your suddenly realizing that the dog has run off (in my case!). However, some people find being at home is even more distracting than being outside, as the doorbell may ring or someone may unexpectedly come into the room. In such instances, you can choose to ignore the doorbell and merely observe it as a sound, but more often than not, you cannot ignore interruptions. Whether indoors or out, it helps to acknowledge that it's impossible to remain undisturbed all the time, so go ahead and respond to the situation and then return to the practice.

PROBLEM SOLVING COMMON DIFFICULTIES WITH MINDFULNESS EXERCISES

If you find yourself struggling with these exercises, your difficulties probably fall into one of several common areas of concern.

Recurring Thoughts and Images

As mentioned previously, during any exercise or practice, our attention may be drawn toward any number of things. Sometimes it will be a sound and we may start to wonder where it came from, or we may start to think about what we are going to have for dinner, or we may reflect on what a nice day it was yesterday. However, sometimes we may notice our minds repeatedly going to a specific situation, past, present, or future, or a particular worry or rumination.

If you have this experience, it may be helpful to make this the focus of some of the later exercises covered in this book. For the time being, maybe just jot down the difficulties you are having. You can then refer back to them.

What to Do If You Feel Intense Emotions

People sometimes experience intense emotions when they practice mindfulness; it is as though the process clears a space into which hidden, bottled up, or suppressed emotions can move. This makes sense, for most people keep themselves or their minds busy so they can avoid dealing with more difficult things.

If your emotions are manageable, then just view them with curiosity and nonjudgment and return to the exercise. You may find that one of the anchoring practices helps here. If, however, the emotions feel more intense, making your practice difficult to return to, maybe just allow yourself to sit with the emotion for a while and experience it. Strong emotions can feel frightening and uncomfortable, but they do subside. Often, allowing ourselves to experience intense emotions, such as sadness and anger, and then feeling them fade away can actually be a healing process.

Again, you may find some later exercises to be helpful in this respect, so you may choose to move on to these now rather than work straight through the book. If you choose to do this, it would be a good idea to return to this section at a later date.

What to Do If Your Mind Is Racing

Hopefully when you become aware of intrusive thoughts, images, or bodily sensations, you will simply reflect that your mind has switched focus and then bring it back to the exercise. However, we all have times when mindfulness and similar practices become more difficult. Usually these experiences are associated with strong emotions that seem to get in the way. Funny enough, these are often the times we most need to practice.

At the start of the book, I mentioned that it is best to start this work when things are relatively easy for you. However, if you find that you are some way into your practice and suddenly things aren't easy, or, alternatively, there never is an easy time, you may want to try one or more of the following:

1. Engage in the exercise accepting without criticism that our brains "have a mind of their own" that we simply cannot control absolutely.

2. If you are criticizing yourself or becoming frustrated, treat this in the same way, observing it and then returning to the exercise.

3. Engage with the exercise fleetingly, despite the distractions. You may be surprised to find just how helpful even snatched moments can be.

4. Write down the things that are on your mind before you begin, and then attempt to leave those things behind on the paper while you do the exercise. It is often interesting how much easier it is to think through things after we do a mindfulness practice.

5. It may be that some of the later exercises in this book will be of greater benefit to you, so move on to those.

HOW TO DEVELOP A MINDFULNESS SELF-PRACTICE

As you experiment with the mindfulness exercises in this chapter, you probably will find that some work better for you than others. You may want to practice regularly with those that you find most helpful, trying them on for size, with the idea of a future self-practice in mind. Practicing them for a week or so before continuing with the rest of this book may be helpful. If, however, you are eager to continue practicing these exercises, you can do so as you read further.

Once you have a feel for what mindfulness is, you can begin to play around with introducing mindfulness to other areas of your life. Here are some examples:

*   Michelle Cree, who is a clinical psychologist working with pregnant women and new mothers, suggests *mindful hand washing* as a way of regularly building mindfulness into a busy day. This

exercise involves being mindful of the feel of water on the skin, the sound of running water, and the smell of soap.

- Susan Albers, in her 2006 book *Mindful Eating*, advocates using mindfulness in a number of ways in relation to food. Modern life means that we often eat while sitting in front of the TV or on the go, either of which can prevent us from really appreciating the texture, taste, and smell of our food. Mindful attention to the food we eat can help us appreciate it more and lead to a better relationship with it and with ourselves.

- In compassion-focused therapy groups, I encourage people to practice mindfulness whenever they drink a cup of tea or coffee. Drinking mindfully is a very different experience from drinking while sitting in front of a computer screen or watching TV. People most commonly report that in practicing such mindful drinking, their brain gets a break from the worries and ruminations that usually occupy their minds. This practice is also a good reminder to integrate other aspects of the compassionate-mind approach into your everyday life.

In short, mindfulness practice can be done for long or short intervals, inside or outside, as part of another activity or as an activity in its own right, in a busy or peaceful place, day or night.

Finally, while some may find that it is easy to be motivated to do ten to fifteen minutes of mindfulness practice per day, others find a note on the fridge or a pebble in the pocket reminds them to engage in self-practice. In the Mindfulness in Schools Project, based in the United Kingdom, high school children were asked to buddy up and randomly text each other once a day the message ".b." This stands for "Stop…breathe." Participants reported this to be a really effective way of bringing mindfulness into their everyday lives.

Maybe you can ask a friend or relative to practice mindfulness also, and then you can experiment with supporting each other through text messages. As with any of these exercises, what's important is finding something that works for you.

CONCLUSIONS

Mindfulness practices have been found by many to be hugely beneficial in their own right, and hopefully this will be the case for you. If you wish to pursue mindfulness practice further, there are many excellent books you may wish to read, a number of which are listed in the resources section.

The compassionate-mind approach encourages you to engage in some form of mindfulness to provide you with a space in or foundation on which you can build self-compassion and through this develop your self-confidence.

8

Further Preparation
for Compassion

Health is the greatest possession. Contentment is the
greatest treasure. Confidence is the greatest friend.

—Lao Tzu

The practice of mindfulness outlined in chapter 7 aims to bring you
to a state of calm awareness, which has curiosity and nonjudgment.
Mindfulness practice brings awareness to the present moment and,
when we notice our attention wandering, observes where our attention
has gone and gently returns it to the practice.

Although not a direct aim of mindfulness, people often report
feeling a sense of warmth, contentment, or soothing during their mindfulness practice. This chapter will focus on nurturing this feeling.

DEVELOPING YOUR SOOTHING SYSTEM

This section will introduce two exercises. The first is a soothing-rhythm breathing exercise, which aims to evoke and develop your own natural capacity for self-soothing. As with any of the exercises, if you find it difficult, try for a little while, but, ultimately, do not continue with anything that seems to have an adverse effect on you, that is, if it results in difficult emotions rather than a soothing and calming experience. There are a large number of exercises in this book that you can use instead. In the compassionate-mind approach, you need not succeed in one exercise before you move on to the next.

The second exercise uses imagery as a means of creating a sensory experience, and the goal is to develop a personal place of contentment created in your own mind. Again, if this is difficult for you, there are some further ideas that may help you later in this chapter.

Both exercises are listed on the personal practice summary sheet at the end of the preface. You can use this sheet, as well as your notebook or journal, to record your reflections.

Exercise 25: Soothing-Rhythm Breathing

Soothing-rhythm breathing is a specific breathing practice that aims to switch on and develop your soothing system. The exercise is designed to help you find your own soothing rhythm. For many, this often involves slowing your breathing to a comfortable, deep, and regular rate. Unlike some forms of relaxation training, it does not require you to adopt a specific pace; rather, it is about finding a pace that is right for you. It also includes an element of mindfulness. During this exercise, when you notice your awareness has moved to something else, be mindful of where it has gone and gently bring it back to your breathing.

To help you concentrate, you may pick something to focus on, such as your nostrils, your chest or rib cage, or counting breaths in, pausing and then counting them out, or a combination of these things. You may already have an idea of what helps, based on the mindfulness-of-breathing exercise in chapter 7, but this exercise will help you explore this idea further.

Start by finding a place that is, as far as possible, free from major distractions, somewhere you can be for ten to fifteen minutes. If you can, sit with an upright posture, feet on the floor hip-distance apart, hands gently resting on your lap. Feel a strength in your spine, yet a relaxation in your body and a sense of openness. It is helpful if you can close your eyes for this exercise, but you may prefer to settle your gaze on a low fixed point.

Sit quietly for a moment and bring your attention to your breathing... noticing the air going in and out though your nose...maybe being aware of the rise and fall of your belly...gradually rising and slowly falling...maybe being aware of your chest rising and falling...aware of your rib cage expanding then contracting. It may help to breathe in to your own count of three...pausing and then exhaling, again to a count of three...finding a breathing pattern that, for you, seems to be your own soothing, comforting rhythm.

Maybe experimenting a little with your breathing...breathing a little faster and then a little slower, and noticing the difference in how your body feels. Once you have found a soothing rhythm, experience it for a few minutes...allowing the air to come into your body slowly and evenly, and then leave it...slowly and evenly, in a breathing rhythm that is soothing for you.

When you are ready, gently bring your awareness to the end of the exercise, becoming more aware of your physical environment. Now it is time for reflection.

Using Your Sense of Smell

Some people find the soothing-rhythm breathing exercise difficult, if not virtually impossible. Pairing this exercise with a soothing smell can sometimes be extremely helpful. The smell could be that of a perfume or aftershave, soap, moisturizer, essential oil, or anything that you find soothing. You can choose a scent with no associations for you or one that has positive memories attached to it. There is a good reason people find this helpful. Our olfactory receptors are connected to the limbic system, thought to be the home of emotion. Unpleasant smells can therefore very quickly trigger our threat system and a fast-acting emotional experience of anxiety, anger, or repulsion. In contrast, pleasant smells can have a fast-acting, positive emotional response, bringing online our contentment and soothing system.

Reflection on Exercise 25

For many, the soothing-rhythm breathing exercise feels quite different from the mindfulness-of-breathing exercise in chapter 7. This is because, in soothing-rhythm breathing, you are focusing on activating your soothing system, in contrast to previous exercises where the primary aim was to bring calm awareness of the moment as it occurs.

If you were able to find your own soothing rhythm as you breathe, you may have noticed how it affects the way you experience thoughts and images that pop into your mind. The relationship with your internal world is likely to change if you are in a soothed state of mind.

It is important to point out that achieving any specific emotional or physical state is not the goal of this exercise. Instead, this exercise is designed to help you switch on your soothing system. Once this is activated, your emotional or physical state probably will alter as a consequence, but this is not the primary aim. Remember, it's not the destination but the journey that counts. Spend too long thinking about a desired outcome, and you will disrupt the practice.

As with the earlier mindfulness exercises, once you have experienced and practiced using your soothing-rhythm breathing, you can then develop your own self-practice. You may, for example, choose to engage with your soothing-rhythm breathing at certain set times in the week. You may decide to practice it while walking, during a coffee break, or in the shower or bath.

Exercise 26: Finding Your Place of Contentment

The purpose of this exercise is to evoke a sense of contentment. This will then be used as a further platform on which to build your self-compassion and self-confidence. Here imagery is used to create a broader sensory experience. Your own place of contentment may be an idealized version of somewhere that is real or a place that is purely imaginary. Alternatively, it may be a combination of different places. This place is devoid of anything threatening. It is a place that always welcomes you.

Once again, this exercise includes an element of mindfulness. Remember, when you become mindful that your awareness has moved to something else, notice where it has gone and gently bring it back to the exercise.

While some people find it helpful to embark on this exercise in a spirit of curiosity as to where they will end up, others find it helpful to do some preparation around an initial image from which they will begin to explore. Still others find that it is helpful to think about what kind of place they are going to steer their minds toward. If you think it may be beneficial for you, take some time to think about the types of places in which you feel or have felt a sense of contentment. Maybe there was a particular picture you felt was warm and inviting. Images often generated by people are of a beach, a wood, or of being in a warm house in front of an open fire. In preparation, you may ask yourself whether you are outside or inside. What smells and sounds are around you? Can you hear the birds, the wind in the trees, or a crackling fire? Can you smell burning wood, freshly cut grass, or water gently lapping against the sides of a boat or on the shore? Would you be looking out from a beach hut or a cabin onto an expanse of ocean or woodland? What would the weather be like? What colors would there be around you?

If your mind goes to a real place, it may be helpful to ask yourself whether that place has any negative connotations attached to it. For example, a childhood bedroom may seem to be an ideal spot to think about as a place of contentment, but if you sometimes felt uncomfortable in your childhood bedroom, it may also conjure up difficult memories and emotions that would distract you from the purpose of this exercise. You could, however, pick aspects of the room, things that made you feel secure and content, and then blend them with other things. Like a designer, you can pick and choose how you want your place of contentment to look. Remember, this is your idealized place.

Ideas to Help with Imagery

While some people find it very easy to conjure up images, it is quite normal to find this difficult. If you find it difficult, here are a few things that other people have found helpful:

- Imagine a color around you, maybe in the form of mist, maybe a blanket.

- Find a photo, a drawing, or a painting that you can focus on and feel your way into.

- Imagine a channel of warm light flowing into and out of your body, from the crown of your head to the tips of your toes.

- Find a piece of soothing music that gives you a sense of contentment.

- Experiment with different smells and see if any of them can evoke a sense of contentment.

There are no rights and wrongs. What's important is gaining a sense of the experience and then developing it further.

It is important to find something that works for you personally. It is also true that what works for you in one situation may not in another, so find something that is right for you at this moment in time.

Once again, start by finding a place that is, as far as possible, free from distractions, a place where you can be peacefully for ten to fifteen minutes. Seat yourself comfortably, feeling strength in your spine, yet relaxation in your body and a sense of openness. It may help to close your eyes, or you may prefer to settle your gaze on a low fixed point.

If you find it helpful, start by using your soothing-rhythm breathing. Alternatively, use one of the other mindfulness practices from chapter 7 to create a sense of calm awareness. Or you may prefer to go straight into the exercise.

When you feel ready, begin to create a place in your mind...a place in which you can experience a sense of contentment and calmness...you may be focusing on a picture or an image you have thought about previously...you could simply be waiting to see where your mind takes you.

As you begin to develop a fleeting impression of what the place will be like, you will now explore what your senses experience in this place… what can you see?…maybe objects, maybe vegetation or animals, maybe an expanse of water or a beach…what colors can you see?…what sounds can you hear?…maybe the rustling of leaves, a breeze, water…maybe the faint sound of music, muffled noises, the distant sound of children laughing, birds singing…how does the air feel?…is it warm or cold?…do you feel the sun on your skin?…are there any smells that you notice?…maybe the scent of grass or the saltiness of the ocean…maybe a waft of scent or the smell of bread. Think about your place of contentment and explore it with all your senses…maybe staying with one place for a while if you find it soothing.

Your wandering mind will take your attention away from this place… when you become mindful that it has wandered, notice where it has moved to and gently return your attention to that part of the experience you find most associated with a sense of contentment, and then continue.

Imagine yourself in the image…what is supporting your body? Maybe the ground is contoured perfectly against it…maybe you are sitting on a cool rock, a cozy bed, or warm sand. Become aware of your own warm facial expression, maybe a half smile, a content gaze.

Now, experience the knowledge that this place welcomes you… its sole purpose is to help you experience a sense of contentment and warmth…it is in harmony with you.

When you are ready, gently bring the exercise to an end and become more aware of your physical environment.

A Note about Your Place of Contentment

A place of contentment may be different from a safe place, although both can evoke very similar sensory experiences. Within this book, I intentionally avoid classic safe-place imagery, preferring instead to use the term *place of contentment*, as this latter option seems less fraught with opportunity for the threat system to muscle in on the experience. More specifically, some people report that use of the term *safe* conjures up contradictory elements of threat. Others report that they can experience a feeling of being safe only in the context of threat—whatever they are safe from—therefore, inadvertently evoking the threat system. As such, people sometimes report a menacing element to a safe place, maybe on the fringes, seeing or sensing another person or the critical part of themselves.

I do, however, use the term *safe place* at times. For some, creating a safe place, which has defenses against threat, may be a necessary stepping-stone to evoking your sense of contentment. For example, someone may initially imagine herself in a safe place cocooned from threat by a magical blanket or a force field. Others may imagine that they are in a bunker ten yards underground. Hopefully, with time and practice, the experience will evolve to one where there is no need for such precautions, just a place that is welcoming and devoid of all threats. As with any of these exercises, there is no right or wrong way of doing things. What's important is finding something that works for you and brings your own soothing system online.

Reflection on Exercise 26

It may be that you will need to do this exercise a number of times before a helpful image comes to mind.

Your place of contentment is personal to you, and therefore you can adapt it as your needs change; it is not fixed.

Even when people settle on a particular image or experience, many of them report that they appreciate a fluidity to it rather than having it remain static like a photo. It would seem that allowing the images to be fluid prevents them from growing overfamiliar with their place of contentment and losing the richness of the experience over time.

Whereas some people do not object to hearing background sounds during these exercises, others find it more difficult. What's important is what evokes a sense of contentment in you. A further thing that people sometimes find difficult is the idea that the place "welcomes" you. In the compassionate-mind approach, we think that this is an important (though not essential) component of the practice, as it often enhances the stimulation of the soothing system. Remember, we can soothe ourselves, but we can also be soothed by others. As your place welcomes you, it becomes a soothing agent.

As noted at the start of this exercise, you are being encouraged, wherever possible, to adopt a posture that has strength and openness in it. This is especially important during this exercise, as many people find that they can become extremely relaxed, to the point of falling asleep. Later, it may be of benefit to use this exercise as a method to help you sleep. However, here you are using it as a foundation for other things that will empower you and build your self-confidence, and if you are going to do this, it helps to remain alert and strong rather than sleepy!

CONCLUSIONS

This chapter has introduced to your mindfulness practice two further exercises that are designed specifically to help you access your soothing system. Mindfulness here is the means by which we focus on the soothing aspect of the practice. Of course, you may also wish to explore other aspects of mindfulness.

Although these exercises involve quite a lot of "doing," you may be itching to do more specifically to build your self-confidence. This may be your drive and resource acquisition system at play. It is important to emphasize, however, that this work is likely to have a positive impact on your self-confidence. Mindfulness can help you disengage from your threat system and difficult thoughts, images, and emotions, while the soothing-rhythm breathing and place-of-contentment exercises bring your soothing system online to help you regulate or tone down your threat system.

9

Developing Your Compassionate Mind

Life isn't about finding yourself. Life is about creating yourself.

—George Bernard Shaw

The early chapters of this book looked in some detail at self-confidence, made a case for building it, and explained the evolutionary origins of our emotional states and how these relate to self-confidence. After you were introduced to the effects of self-undermining and how self-compassion may help with this, chapter 4 encouraged you to think about your own situation—both the events that led you to the point where you are now and the things that maintain your situation—by means of a formulation or diagram. This hopefully helped address any self-criticism you may experience. Your formulation should also have shown the areas of your life that may be beneficial to address.

The focus of this chapter is on developing your compassionate mindset and, more specifically, the key dimension of *self*-compassion. We will do this through a number of different imagery exercises. While some exercises offer different approaches to achieving the same result, others are distinct. Hopefully, practicing a combination of these exercises will enable you to build up the different aspects of your compassionate mind and, in particular, self-compassion.

Through the compassionate mindset, you can discover new ways of thinking about things, new motivations, new behaviors, and more pleasurable emotions. This mindset will also help you tone down the threat system associated with experiences such as anxiety, anger, and habitual undermining of yourself.

The Importance of Facial Expressions and Posture

Our facial expressions and posture can have a profound effect on the way we feel and how others perceive us. A number of studies have demonstrated that we can consciously manipulate such things to good effect. For example, one study demonstrated that it was possible to manipulate how funny participants found cartoons by instructing them to do one of two things. While looking at the images, the first group was told to hold a pencil between their teeth, ensuring that it did not touch their lips. The second group was told to hold the pencil in their mouths, without it touching their teeth. The former group "enjoyed" or found the cartoons funnier than the second group. This was attributed to the smile that was elicited by the first facial position (using teeth only). We also know that people who have smiles on their faces are considered by others to be warmer and more approachable. Therefore, smiling can make us enjoy things more and make us more likely to have positive interactions with others.

Similarly, and something that has been practiced by method actors for decades, we can manipulate our posture as a way of evoking particular emotions. Posture can also influence the way we think, what we pay attention to, and how our bodies feel. For example, if you were to walk down the street with your shoulders sagging, dragging your feet, and lowering your gaze, it would be likely to have an impact on your mood, your thoughts, and how you felt physically. However, if you were to walk with strength in your spine, shoulders back, with an inquisitive gaze, and a bounce in your step, your mood would be likely to reflect this with positive thoughts. You also would probably feel better physically. If this posture were combined with an open and warm facial expression, others would probably see you as more approachable.

All of this is so important, for if we wait to do something until we feel like it, we can be waiting a long time. Sometimes it is about doing something despite not feeling like it and manipulating our posture and facial expression to help us do it. It's not about kidding yourself but about giving yourself a helping hand.

DEVELOPING DIFFERENT ASPECTS OF YOUR COMPASSIONATE MINDSET

It is intended that the following exercises will form the basis of your future self-practice and that you will use them throughout the rest of your life to enhance your own well-being. Since you will be returning to them frequently, it may be worthwhile spending some time recording yourself reading them aloud so that you can follow them with minimal disturbance. Alternatively, sound files of each of these exercises can be found on the Compassionate Mind Foundation website (www.compassionatemind.co.uk).

What Is Self-Compassion?

Chapter 5 defined compassion as a mentality, or a mindset, with certain attributes, such as empathy, nonjudgment, and distress tolerance, that are practiced in the context of warmth. Self-compassion involves experiencing these things in relation to yourself and your experiences. In addition, in some of the exercises in this chapter, you will be encouraged to employ the following qualities:

Wisdom: The wisdom of self-compassion tells us that where we find ourselves today is not our fault. Our complicated brains are the product of evolution and are equipped with a need for nurturing, have a "better safe than sorry" default setting, and are home to all manner of conflicting emotions and drives. Our brains are further shaped by experiences throughout our lives, and all of this leads us to behave, think, and feel in certain ways.

Strength, fortitude, and courage: These qualities give us an inner strength and confidence to face the things we need to face, often despite our threat system urging us to avoid or ignore a per-ceived danger. If we are self-compassionate, we can place ourselves in situations knowing that, no matter what, we will be okay.

Responsibility: This involves recognizing that, although some-thing is not our fault, we need to make a commitment to ourselves, and sometimes to others, to do our best to resolve the issue. Together with wisdom, strength, and warmth, responsibility helps us face the things we need to address.

Many people initially report that they find it much easier to work on these qualities of self-compassion when they are finding other attributes, such as sympathy and empathy, difficult to practice. So, if certain components of compassion are hard for you at first, start with what is easy and develop things from there.

Exercise 27: Being Deeply Compassionate

This exercise will help you explore and develop an idea of what com-passion feels like within your mind and body. You will be encouraged to explore a range of different qualities in turn, paying attention to how these feel in your mind and then how they feel in your body. Some people may find this easy, while others may struggle and require additional practice. For the purposes of this exercise, it doesn't matter if you feel you actually possess these qualities or not.

During this exercise it may be helpful for you to think of yourself as an actor. Actors aren't required to have personal experience of everything they represent, but instead to "try on" the experience and embody it. While "getting into character," they stimulate certain qualities in their minds and bodies. They are then able to inhabit the character and become the person they are attempting to portray. Try to approach this exercise in the same way.

Before you begin, start by finding a place that is, as far as possible, free from distractions, somewhere you can be for ten to fifteen minutes. Sit in a relaxed, open posture with strength or alertness to it. It is helpful if you can close your eyes for this exercise, but you may prefer to settle your gaze on a low fixed point.

You may want to embark upon any of the exercises in this chapter by first using your soothing-rhythm breathing or place-of-contentment exercise. Alternatively, use one of the mindfulness practices to create a sense of calm awareness, or else simply go straight into an exercise after your mind and body are settled. Remember, there are no rights and wrongs in the compassionate-mind approach.

Now imagine you are a deeply compassionate person. Experience what it feels like....how does it feel in your mind and in your body?...maybe you find that you sit differently or experience your body differently...maybe your facial expression changes when you step into the role of a deeply compassionate person. It may be that this does not come automatically and you need to change your posture or your expression intentionally. This is okay. What's important is that you get a sense of what it feels like to be a deeply compassionate person.

Wisdom tells us that we all just find ourselves here...we are the product of our genes and our nurture...this is not our fault...it is something we have no control over...for a moment, experience how it feels, in your mind and in your body, to know this.

Now, feeling strength...fortitude...courage in your mind...how does that feel now in your body? Maybe you find that you sit differently or experience your body differently...maybe it helps to adjust your posture in order to help yourself feel these things.

Now, with the experience of wisdom, strength, fortitude, and courage, experience the quality of warmth...how does that feel in your mind?...how does it feel in your body? Imagine yourself speaking to someone and hearing the warm tone of your voice.

Experience within your mind how it feels to hold a commitment to address things in a compassionate way...now feel it within your body...a motivation to face difficulties and increase well-being through compassion.

When you are ready, gently bring your awareness to the end of the exercise, becoming more aware of your physical environment.

Settling Your Mind and Body

In chapters 7 and 8, you were encouraged to explore mindfulness, soothing-rhythm breathing, and a place of contentment. Through the process of engaging with such exercises, it is likely that you developed your own way of settling your mind and body before you began. When prompted, engage in those things that you find to be helpful.

Reflection on Exercise 27

As this is the first exercise that looks specifically at the experience of compassion, you may find it challenging and require further practice before you feel you can recognize the feeling within your mind and body.

Although the compassionate-mind approach aims to create a compassionate mindset, it also pays particular attention to the associated physical sensations, because mind and body are closely connected. Our mindset affects the way we feel physically. For example, if we are in a threat mindset, our stomachs may churn, we may feel sick, tense, experience a sensation of pins and needles, or feel chest pain. The focus of our attention may turn to the way our bodies are feeling, and this may further increase the sense of threat. By contrast, in a compassionate mindset, we are likely to feel a sense of relaxed alertness, warmth, and strength in both mind and body. Hopefully, paying equal attention to each will create in you an enhanced sense of compassion.

You may have found that your posture and expression changed slightly during the exercise, or you may consciously have tried to change them. Some people report that with a change of posture they gain an increased sense of relaxation and warmth, together with more strength and alertness. Others say that they find they sit up straighter and develop a more relaxed facial expression, maybe with a half smile or a sense of warmth in their eyes (even if they are closed).

Exercise 28: Reexperiencing Your Own Compassion

Before doing this exercise, it may be helpful to spend a little time bringing to mind an occasion when you felt a sense of compassion or acted in a compassionate way. Try not to concentrate on a situation that could be charged with very strong emotions, as this may raise all sorts of confusing feelings within you. Instead, start with something that is neither charged with strong emotions nor devoid of them. Usually people find that it is easier to think about a situation where they felt compassion toward someone else than it is to recall a situation where they felt compassion toward themselves. Maybe you can remember a time when you helped someone in need: a child who was hurt or someone who was going through a difficult time.

Find a place where you can be for ten to fifteen minutes that is, as far as possible, free from distractions. Sit in a relaxed, open posture that has strength or alertness in it. Close your eyes or settle your gaze on a low fixed point.

Now bring to mind a time when you felt compassion toward someone or acted in a compassionate way...recalling the event and thinking yourself into the situation...how do you experience compassion in your mind?... how does it feel in your body?...maybe you feel a sense of warmth, of strength, or an urge to move toward the individual...what facial expression does it evoke?...what posture does it move you into?...if you spoke, what would your tone of voice be like?

Experiencing the sense of caring for the other person's well-being... being moved by that person's experience...being motivated to do what you believe will help him or her...being able to witness and tolerate the other person's distress, not turn away...being sensitive to that person without judgment...feeling a strong motivation to alleviate that person's distress.

When you are ready, gently bring the exercise to an end and become more aware of your physical environment.

Reflection on Exercise 28

This exercise can be an extremely powerful way of highlighting our own natural compassion. It can also help to analyze the experience of compassion. We often view the outcome of a situation as the only part of it worth noting. By recalling all the different elements of this exercise, you can give yourself a better and more in-depth understanding of how the process of compassion feels.

If you were recalling an emotionally charged situation, it may stimulate thoughts in you of what happened previously or subsequently. If this is the case, either attempt to focus on the compassionate component and be mindful of when your mind wanders to other things, or else try the exercise again while recalling a different experience, one that is less clouded by other associations.

You may wonder why you are doing this exercise if you have no problem feeling compassionate toward others. Indeed, many people find that they fall into the trap of being so compassionate to others that it is to their own detriment. The purpose of this exercise is not to develop in you compassion for others but to let you explore how compassion *feels* through reflecting on the experience of compassion for others. This will help later when you start to develop self-compassion.

Exercise 29: The Ideal Compassionate Self

Find a place where you can be for ten to fifteen minutes that is, as far as possible, free from distractions. Sit in a relaxed, open posture that has strength or alertness in it. Close your eyes or settle your gaze on a low fixed point.

Now, for a moment, imagine that a self-supporting or compassionate part of you could be thought of as a person. Spend a few moments imagining and experiencing this. Now imagine becoming that person...move into and assume the role just as an actor steps into a part...a compassionate ideal...devoid of human preoccupations and conflicts.

How does this feel in your body?...how do you experience it in your mind?...what is the posture of your ideal compassionate self?...what is your facial expression?...if you were able to look at your ideal compassionate self, what would it look like?...old or young?...large or small?...are there colors or particular smells that come to mind associated with this image?... do you feel a sense of warmth?

In the role of your ideal compassionate self, experience a pure sensation of caring for well-being...experiencing sympathy...empathy...tolerance of distress...being sensitive and nonjudgmental. Feel the wisdom of your ideal compassionate self...the warmth...the strength and courage...feel the commitment to resolving difficulties and moving toward well-being.

Remember, this is an ideal compassionate self, devoid of human preoccupations and conflicts, feeling yourself into this role.

When you are ready, gently end the exercise and become more aware of your physical environment.

Reflection on Exercise 29

It is important to remember that the purpose of this exercise is to assume the role of an ideal, compassionate self. No human individual can be free from feelings of conflict, struggles, and disappointments, because these are what make us human. Drives and desires, "better safe than sorry" thinking, our physical needs, and all manner of other things constantly compete for attention within our minds and bodies. We may wish to maintain the qualities of compassion but find it impossible. However, we can develop and enhance the capacity to be compassionate toward ourselves, and all of the things that make us human, with practice.

You may have noticed your ideal compassionate self as being older than you, in some way softer; you may have felt a sense of warmth and ease in its presence.

As with any of these exercises, when you notice your mind has wandered, note where it has been drawn and then gently and warmly bring it back to the exercise.

Exercise 30: Evoking a Memory of Compassion from Others

In an ideal world, we learn to be soothing to ourselves through initially receiving soothing from others. A child who has been regularly soothed by a parent over time learns to internalize this and eventually is able to do it for himself or herself. This means that if you experience a strong reaction to a difficult event, you can calm yourself down, accept help from others, and ultimately feel better about a situation over time.

But for some people the ability to soothe themselves is underdeveloped. Whether this is true for you, or if you simply need to maintain or enhance your ability to self-soothe, the following exercise may be of benefit to you.

In preparation, bring to mind the memory of an occasion when someone was there for you. This person knew exactly what you needed at the time, be it a hug, a sympathetic ear when you wanted to talk or rant, or maybe simply supporting you by being present. A time when someone was sensitive to your distress, strong, nonjudgmental, and had your well-being at heart. A time when you felt a deep sense of connection with someone.

Try to avoid choosing a memory that is closely linked to a very strong or difficult emotion. This can happen if we think about, for example, someone who has died or whom we no longer see, or if we think about a really distressing time in our lives, something that is always likely to arouse strong emotion in us. This is not to say that it may not be helpful, at some future time, to reflect on such events, but for the purposes of this exercise, it is better to start with something easier. Find a place where you can be for ten to fifteen minutes that is, as far as possible, free from distractions. Sit in a relaxed, open posture that has strength or alertness in it. Close your eyes or settle your gaze on a low fixed point.

Now bring to mind an experience when you felt a deep sense of connection with someone...a time when you were struggling and this person was compassionate toward you...who knew exactly what you needed and did it...maybe was sympathetic and nonjudgmental...wise and strong... sensitive to your situation and tolerant of your distress.

Bring to mind the person's facial expression and maybe posture... bring to mind the environment you were in and what it looked like...what it smelled like...bring to mind the sounds around you, maybe the tone of the person's voice...if the person hugged you, what did it feel like?...if this person touched your arm or gave you a reassuring nod, how did that feel? Recall how somebody's compassion for you felt...in both your mind and body.

Spend time evoking the memory and experiencing it. When you are ready, gently bring the exercise to an end and become more aware of your physical environment.

Reflection on Exercise 30

There is no universal pattern of compassionate behavior. For some, in the moment, it's a hug or a compassionate gaze in which they know that the other person is there for them; for others it's having their minds taken away from a difficult time, but once again with the knowledge that the other person is motivated by their best interests. For most people it is a mixture of these things at different times. What is common, however, is the sensation of the other person doing for you exactly what you need at that time.

Memories of real events can be extremely powerful in evoking a sense of connectedness to others, a sense of not being on your own. Unfortunately, depression and anxiety can sometimes make it difficult for us to bring to mind such positive memories; instead we recall anxiety-provoking or depressing events. Others may simply lack positive memories to call upon. If either of these cases applies to you, it may help to try recalling a friend at school, a kindly teacher, or a supportive colleague. It need not be someone you knew for a long time.

If you can find one positive memory and use this exercise in conjunction with it, you may find that it helps you recall others. Such memories may pop into your mind during or after you have finished this exercise. Jot down any new memories so you can use them later.

Whether recalling such a memory was easy or proved to be more difficult, if you found this exercise helpful, it may be useful to repeat it using other memories.

In the next two exercises, you will turn compassion outward, toward others and then toward someone who struggles with self-confidence. This will be a further step toward learning how to be compassionate toward yourself and your own situation.

Ultimately you are hoping to develop self-compassion for your own struggles with self-confidence as an antidote to self-criticism and a source of future strength and resilience. From this mindset, you can then coach yourself in the building of your self-confidence like an encouraging, supportive teacher.

Exercise 31: Turning Compassion Outward

In preparation for this exercise, bring to mind someone you care about who is going through some form of difficulty at the moment. It could be a friend, relative, or partner. Use this person as the focus of your compassion. Once again, be careful not to think about someone who is likely to bring up difficult emotions, such as someone you can no longer be with or someone who is experiencing acute difficulties at the moment.

Find a place where you can be for ten to fifteen minutes that is, as far as possible, free from distractions. Sit in a relaxed, open posture that has strength or alertness in it. Close your eyes or settle your gaze on a low fixed point.

Reminding yourself of the compassionate mind's attributes and qualities...experience a pure sense of care for well-being...sympathy... empathy...tolerance of distress...sensitivity and nonjudgment...feel the wisdom of your compassionate mind...the warmth...the strength and courage...feel the commitment to resolve difficulties and move toward well-being...feel these qualities in both your mind and your body.

Now bringing to mind the person you wish to direct compassion toward...experience your own compassion toward this person...experience a pure sense of care for his or her well-being...sympathy and empathy... tolerance of distress...sensitivity and nonjudgment. Feel the wisdom of your compassionate mind...the warmth...the strength and courage...feel the commitment to help to resolve this person's difficulties and let him or her move toward well-being...feel these qualities in both your mind and body.

When you are ready, gently bring the exercise to an end and become more aware of your physical environment.

Reflection on Exercise 31

People often find during this exercise that their minds will wander with thoughts of, for example, when they are going to see this particular person next, what they did last time they saw this person, or what they are doing now. This is perfectly normal. What is important is noticing when your mind has wandered from the exercise, being mindful of where it has gone, and gently bringing it back.

You may experience a heightened sense of emotion. This is because cells in your brain named *mirror neurons* are firing and giving you a strong sense of how the other person must be feeling, as well as a sense of connectedness to him or her. This is why you are encouraged, at least initially, to engage in this exercise by focusing on someone who is not in acute distress.

Once you have practiced compassion for someone you care about in this more general way, you can then attempt to develop compassion specifically toward those who struggle in a similar way to you. This is the focus of the next exercise.

Exercise 32: Compassion for Those Who Lack Self-Confidence

This exercise will involve directing your compassionate mind toward someone who may be similar to you in that he or she lacks self-confidence.

In preparation, think about someone who you think lacks self-confidence. It may be a person you know well, someone you know merely by sight, or someone in the public eye. You may choose someone who lacks self-confidence in every area of life or in just one area, and to a greater or a lesser extent.

Find a place where you can be for ten to fifteen minutes that is, as far as possible, free from distractions. Sit in a relaxed, open posture that has strength or alertness in it. Close your eyes or settle your gaze on a low fixed point

Reminding yourself of the compassionate mind's qualities...experience a pure sense of care for well-being...sympathy...empathy...tolerance of distress...sensitivity and nonjudgment...feel the wisdom of your compassionate mind...the warmth...the strength and courage...feel the commitment to resolve difficulties and move toward well-being...feel these qualities in both your mind and body.

Now bring to mind someone who is lacking in self-confidence and direct those compassionate qualities toward this person...consider the things that may have contributed to his or her difficulties...consider the effort he or she needs to put into getting through situations others seem to find easy...consider the impact of his or her lack of self-confidence...the things this person has and hasn't done...the traps he or she has encountered. Now think about what this person needs to overcome his or her difficulties...strength and courage...tolerance of inevitable distress...sympathy and empathy for his or her own situation...self-support as opposed to judgment and self-criticism.

If you find it difficult to feel compassion, that is okay...maybe instead focus on your own behavior toward the other person and your good intentions toward this person...maybe the compassionate feelings will come later.

Focus your compassionate mind and all its key qualities on that person for a few minutes.

When you are ready, gently bring the exercise to an end and become more aware of your physical environment.

Reflection on Exercise 32

While some people find this exercise extremely easy, others find it incredibly difficult. Some people find that despite feeling an almost total lack of compassion for themselves and a high level of self-criticism, they can easily be compassionate toward others in a similar position.́ Although compassion for others is important, it can be problematic if we do not have equal compassion for ourselves too.

Others find this exercise extremely difficult because they see themselves in the person they are imagining, and this may lead to their becoming critical of the other person's situation and struggles. Your self-critic may become very negative toward the subject of this exercise. Whatever the issue is, people can find it difficult to be around others who remind them of their own situation and can find themselves being inadvertently hostile toward fellow sufferers. If this is the case for you, take some reassurance from the fact that it's very common. It does, however, mean that you may need to gently nurture this capacity within yourself, attempting to build it up, just as you are attempting to build your self-confidence. Here are some strategies:

- Engage in the exercise again, and whenever you become mindful of being critical toward the subject, bring your attention back to a mindfulness exercise, soothing-rhythm breathing, or your place of contentment. Once you have done this, engage with your compassionate mind and return to the exercise.

- Focus the exercise on someone who is a little less lacking in self-confidence, maybe focusing on someone who shows a lack of self-confidence in only one area of life.

- Engage in the exercise while focusing compassion on a timid animal. This may seem odd, but the idea is to train your brain ultimately toward developing self-compassion for your own struggles. Where you start does not matter. What matters is where you end up.

Exercise 33: Turning Compassion Inward

In preparation, bring to mind a childhood situation when you struggled with something. It could be with your homework or in a particular class; it could be in a specific social situation or with a particular sport. As with the previous exercises, try not to concentrate on a situation that was charged with strong emotions, as doing this may be counterproductive. Instead, start with something that is neither too charged with emotion nor devoid of it but somewhere in the middle.

Find a place where you can be for ten to fifteen minutes that is, as far as possible, free from distractions. Sit in a relaxed, open posture that has strength or alertness in it. Close your eyes or settle your gaze on a low fixed point.

Settle your mind and body, maybe through your soothing-rhythm breathing, maybe in your place of contentment.

Now open up to your compassionate mind and all the sensory experiences this brings with it...maybe assuming the role of a deeply compassionate person...maybe evoking compassion through a memory...maybe assuming your ideal compassionate self.

Gently bring to mind a situation from childhood when you found yourself struggling...for a moment observe yourself....with your compassionate mind, experience compassion for yourself as that child...care for well-being...sympathy and empathy...ability to tolerate and contain the distress...sensitivity and attention to the distress...nonjudgment...doing all of this in the context of warmth.

When you are ready, gently bring the exercise to an end and become more aware of your physical environment.

Reflection on Exercise 33

This exercise can prove difficult, as it may evoke troubling memories, emotions, thoughts, and feelings. This is why you are asked to do this exercise in relation to a childhood situation. When associated with sadness, childhood memories tend to be less weighted with self-criticism and are consequently easier to view with compassion.

Developing compassion toward one aspect of yourself, at one time in your life, can be a step toward becoming generally more self-compassionate.

Exercise 34: Compassion for Your Own Journey and Situation

In this exercise, you will revisit the formulation you completed in exercise 8 (chapter 4). It is hoped that the work you have done to date will bring a deeper understanding and emotional connectedness to your current situation and journey.

In preparation, look back at your formulation in chapter 4 (see diagram 4). This represented the factors leading up to your current situation and the things that seem to maintain it. It specifically looked at the origins of your lack of self-confidence and what has prevented you from building it.

Now, finding a place where you can be for ten to fifteen minutes that is, as far as possible, free from distractions, sit in a relaxed, open posture that has strength or alertness in it. Close your eyes or settle your gaze on a low fixed point. Settle your mind and body, maybe through your soothing-rhythm breathing or your place-of-contentment exercise.

Awaken your compassionate mind and all the sensory experiences this brings with it...maybe assuming the role of a deeply compassionate person...maybe evoking compassion through a memory...maybe assuming your ideal compassionate self.

Reminding yourself of the compassionate mind's attributes...experience a pure sense of care for well-being...sympathy...empathy...tolerance of distress...sensitivity and nonjudgment...feel the wisdom of your compassionate mind...the warmth...the strength and courage...feel the commitment to resolve difficulties and move toward well-being...feel these qualities in both your mind and body.

Once you have evoked a sense of compassion, no matter how small or however fleeting, open your eyes and slowly, gently, and warmly read through your formulation...take time to reflect on the words and their meaning in turn...staying with each point or sentence until you feel as though you connect with what is written.

Take as much time as you need to read through, reflect, and emotionally absorb what you have written and, most importantly, what you have experienced or continue to experience.

When you feel you are ready, gently end the exercise by becoming more aware of your physical environment.

Reflection on Exercise 34

The purpose of this exercise is to turn your formulation into a more emotional experience. Again, for some this can be done relatively easily, while for others it can be more difficult.

If you are able to develop compassion for past and present circumstances, it is likely that the exercise will have been associated with some degree of emotion. That emotion may be extremely strong, or it may be less so. Maybe you found that you were able to connect emotionally with only some aspects of what you had written, or maybe you were able to connect with the formulation as a whole.

Whether or not this exercise turned your formulation into a more emotional experience, it may be useful to return to it and try it again. Some people find it helpful to rewrite their formulation after completing this exercise, this time using more compassionate language or else adding to it. You will return to your formulation once more and use it in the compassionate letter-writing exercise that appears later in this book, but for the time being, it may be useful to reflect upon the difference that switching to a compassionate mindset makes.

Exercise 35: Developing Your Compassionate Coach

Here you will look at how to develop your compassionate coach, which will help you generate a compassionate mindset.

Your compassionate coach won't be critical or hostile, forever pointing out what you have done wrong and undermining you. Instead, your compassionate coach will work to build your self-confidence in a more helpful and meaningful way. Sometimes it may help you be more understanding of and kinder toward yourself. At other times it may coach you in how to approach external factors, giving you the strength to negotiate the important situations you face and, perhaps more importantly, helping you feel more confident in everyday life too.

You may develop a very detailed mental image of your coach that has the quality of a cartoon or a photograph. Alternatively, your compassionate coach may be merely a hazy impression. It doesn't matter which kind of image you develop; the qualities your coach possesses are what's more important, how he or she coaches you and how you feel in your coach's presence.

Now, finding a place where you can be for ten to fifteen minutes that is, as far as possible, free from distractions, sit in a relaxed, open posture that has strength or alertness in it. Close your eyes or settle your gaze on a low fixed point.

Awakening your compassionate mind and all the sensory experiences this brings with it...maybe assuming the role of a deeply compassionate person...maybe evoking compassion through a memory...maybe assuming the ideal compassionate self...now imagine an ideal compassionate coach...someone who has your best interests at heart...someone who concentrates purely on your well-being.

What kind of qualities would she have? Imagine her being sympathetic to your difficulties...imagine that she always knows what you need... sometimes offering gentle encouragement...sometimes motivating you... other times simply being alongside you in difficult situations...imagine her being tolerant of all the emotions you feel and show...sensitive and nonjudgmental.

Imagine how it feels to be in the presence of your coach's infinite wisdom...warmth...strength and courage...feel your coach's commitment to resolving any difficulties you have and to building your self-confidence.

Spend a short time imagining your compassionate coach...your coach's qualities of compassion...the sensory experience as you receive it...imagine being in your coach's presence and how that feels in your mind and body.

When you feel ready, gently bring the exercise to an end and become aware of your physical environment.

Reflections on Exercise 35

Clear visual images of a coach can range from someone similar to a sports coach to an older woman or man to a teacher, a tree, a fairy, an angel, or even a particular place.

Some find that the image that most easily comes to mind is that of someone they once knew or know now. Where possible, it is helpful to avoid real people, alive or dead, for two reasons. First, human beings are never perfect, and what you are trying to create here is an ideal compassionate coach. Secondly, real people tend to trigger a range of emotions within us, and this may make it difficult for us to focus on the exercise or indeed on pure compassion. If this is the case for you, it may be helpful to blend this image of someone you know with something else to give the coach a nonhuman dimension that allows it to be removed in your mind from anything or anyone else.

Following on from this, you may also find that the term *coach* isn't the right one for you. Ken Goss, in his book *The Compassionate-Mind Guide to Ending Overeating*, uses the idea of an "ideal compassionate companion" while, in her work with those who have experienced trauma, Deborah Lee uses the term "perfect nurturer." Maybe "compassionate teacher" or "compassionate guide" would work better for you. Interestingly, some people find that one image is helpful in a particular situation while another may be more helpful in a different scenario. Some people like to have a mixture of male and female images. Who knows? Play around with the ones that help you most, and you may end up with a whole gang around you! Just concentrate on finding what works best for you.

The Compassionate Coach

Your compassionate coach does not replace the need to have real people around you and to build your self-confidence in relation to them. However, such imagery does have many advantages:

- A compassionate coach can be especially useful to those who do not have supportive people around them.

- A compassionate coach is always available, unlike human beings.

- A compassionate coach can help the way we relate to ourselves and the way we relate to others, thus making it more likely that we will develop meaningful, real relationships.

- A compassionate coach can be a helpful bridge to being more compassionate toward ourselves.

- A compassionate coach can be used to help prepare us for other parts of this compassionate-mind approach, such as taking action and looking at our thoughts, which we will do later in this book.

- A compassionate coach can help us be more mindful and less reactive.

• *Cherokee Story: The Wolves Within*

A Native American elder was teaching his grandchildren about life. He said to them, "A fight occurs within me. It is a terrible fight between two wolves. One wolf represents fear, anger, envy, sorrow, regret, greed, arrogance, self-pity, resentment, inferiority, lies, false pride, superiority, and ego. The other stands for joy, peace, love, hope, sharing, serenity, humility, kindness, benevolence, friendship, empathy, generosity, truth, compassion, and faith. This same fight is going on inside you, and inside every other person too," he added. The grandchildren thought about this for a minute and then one child asked his grandfather, "Which wolf will win?" The old Cherokee paused for a moment and then warmly replied, "The one you feed."

CONCLUSIONS

Once developed, your compassionate mind acts as a foundation on which to build your self-confidence. It can tone down your threat system and equip you with the necessary attributes, skills, and qualities to stand tall and face life's difficulties.

As you are hopefully doing with the mindfulness exercises, attempt to bring the exercises from this chapter into your everyday life. This may involve setting aside some time each day to practice them. Later on, you may find that you set aside specific times less frequently but can instead incorporate these practices easily into your regular routines, engaging in them, for instance, whenever you have a hot drink, while out on a walk, or when watering the plants.

10

Using Compassionate Thinking in Response to Your Own Undermining

The glow of one warm thought is to me worth more than money.

—Thomas Jefferson

You have seen how the mind can become a playground for undermining thoughts, images, and self-criticism. These are frequently accompanied by difficult emotions, a range of physical sensations, and certain accompanying behaviors. This chapter will look at ways to use compassionate thinking to address this tendency to be self-undermining.

Compassionate thinking in relation to self-confidence involves warmly understanding yourself: both the factors that have influenced you in the past and those that influence you in your moment-to-moment living. It involves being empathic to your own difficulties, and it can help you develop the strength and courage to address them.

This chapter will focus on:

- Understanding your thinking and the views you may hold

- Noticing thoughts and images that occur in your mind

- Generating compassionate alternative thoughts and images, and evaluating thoughts that can undermine you from the perspective of both the rational and the compassionate mind

- Using two chairs to strengthen your compassionate mind

UNDERSTANDING YOUR THINKING AND THE VIEWS YOU MAY HOLD

A number of different things can be running through your mind at any one time. Sometimes these thoughts and images can relate to general everyday things, but if you struggle with self-confidence, it is likely that many of your thoughts and images relate to ruminations about things that *have* happened and worries about things that *may* happen. Events in your everyday life can also trigger thoughts about the kind of person you believe you are, as well as how you view others and the world in general.

As if this weren't enough, you can have an additional layer of thoughts about the thoughts themselves. In other words, you may criticize yourself for the way that you think, concluding *There's something wrong with me*, *If only I could think more positively*, or *I must be weird to think like this*.

In preparation for later exercises, the first part of this chapter will examine why we tend to think in certain ways and how our views develop. It will also look at why it may take time to change these patterns of thinking. It will then discuss how you can recruit your new brain to assist you in these efforts.

Our Amazing Brain Capacity Can Be a Double-Edged Sword

As human beings, we have the capacity for complex thought and thoughts about thoughts (often referred to as *metacognition*). This allows us to run a commentary on our everyday lives as events unfold. By way of a narrative or images, we can reflect on past events and predict future ones. All of this has been hugely important for the survival of our species. The human brain has evolved in ways that help us see the links between things, understand other people's behavior and motivations, prepare us for events that we predict, work out risk factors associated with past events, and allow us to shift into the world of our imaginations.

However, our brains also have a "better safe than sorry" factory setting, which can leave us more likely to focus on the things we find difficult (be they in the past, present, or yet to occur) and on trying to work them out. This can generate difficult emotions in us, as well as physical sensations and, of course, accompanying thoughts and images. A key point to remember is that all of this happens through no fault of our own but is the product of our brains and biology plus the life experiences we have had.

Change Occurs Step-by-Step

At times, we can readily change our opinions and thoughts about things. For example, you already might have experienced an epiphany when reading something in this book, which changed your views and thoughts almost immediately.

However, at other times, changing the way we think or how we view ourselves is a more gradual process. Three factors influence this: first, how the brain processes information; second, how much time we have spent thinking in a certain way and therefore training our brains; and third, how long it takes for us to learn something new.

How the Brain Processes Information

Research has shown that to help us navigate the complex world we live in and the constant barrage of information around us, over time the brain has developed a way of drawing snap conclusions and making instantaneous predictions. Its main focus is reserved for more important things. This means that we experience conclusions and predictions in the form of *beliefs* and *assumptions*, and they apply to our physical surroundings and the people within them, as well as to our own physical attributes and the type of person we are. The brain assumes all such beliefs and assumptions to be true. It will readily accept things that confirm its views but can often reject or modify information that is inconsistent with these.

• *Susan's Story*

Susan had grown up being told that she was "useless" and was treated that way by her family. Her mother and father and even her younger siblings would automatically do everything for her, assuming that she was unable to help herself, and would poke fun at her whenever the family got together. She quickly learned to defer to others and accepted her own uselessness as fact. As an adult, whenever she came across situations that confirmed this view, she readily accepted them as further proof or evidence that she was, indeed, useless.

Susan did not recognize her own achievements or personal strengths, and even when she did receive evidence of them, when things went well for her, she would quickly dismiss this by saying it was "only luck," someone was just trying to be nice to her, or, more worryingly, people were trying to manipulate her for their own ends. For example, despite getting a job that she enjoyed upon leaving school and slowly working her way up into management, Susan could not see that her success reflected her own skills or attributes. She attributed it to "being in the right place at the right time" and even wondered whether her mother or father had orchestrated things for her. Upon receiving a promotion, she thought, There's only me available to do the job. If there were any competition, they wouldn't have promoted me.

From Susan's story, you can see how our brains sometimes fix us in a seemingly never-ending pattern that further reinforces the negative way we view ourselves. Changing this pattern takes time and effort.

How Long You Have Been Training Your Brain

If you have been viewing yourself in a certain way all your life, you will have been engaging in this way of thinking for hundreds of thousands of hours. When I consciously started to work on my own self-confidence, I was thirty-four. This meant that I had already been thinking, behaving, and feeling in a particular way about myself for approximately 297,024 hours. Look at the table below to work out how many hours you have spent training your brain so far.

Age	Hours
20	175,200
30	262,800
40	350,400
50	438,000
60	525,600
70	613,200
80	700,800
90	788,400

Of course, you have not been awake for the entire time, and the negative view you have of yourself may have begun as late as your teens or early twenties, but it is worthwhile working out just how many hours you may have spent thinking of yourself in a particular way. If you are shocked by the total, perhaps you now understand why it might take a great deal of time and effort to make fundamental changes.

How Long It Takes to Learn New Skills

Achieving any new skill takes time and effort, which is why compassion-focused therapy or the compassionate-mind approach is often referred to as physiotherapy for the brain. We build up to changing things, step-by-step.

The exercises in this book can actually produce long-term changes in the brain, but such *new brain* pathways can be difficult to develop and use at first, just as you may find it difficult to find a path through the woods that has been walked only a few times before. Other pathways, such as self-critical ones, can be easier to find, but you know what happens if you follow only those. The action you most need to take is to repeatedly and purposefully walk the new pathways, which will in time make these paths easier to find and follow. The aim is to make the new pathways more attractive than the old ones until, all of a sudden, you find that you no longer have to make a conscious effort to switch to them. Following the path of change becomes automatic.

HOW YOU CAN RECRUIT YOUR NEW BRAIN TO ASSIST YOU

The good news is that your new brain has the capacity to reason with the old one and, where appropriate, calm it down or soothe it. More specifically, you can use your new brain to allow yourself to step back from your own unruly mind and gain a better perspective on what is happening. You can reevaluate situations using your new brain, often leading to different responses, different ways of viewing things, and different emotions.

Noticing Thoughts and Images That Occur in Your Mind

Some people find that they are already very aware of the thoughts and images that occupy their minds and undermine their self-confidence. If this is the case for you, you may choose to skip the next two exercises, proceeding straight to exercise 38. However, if you find it difficult to identify or describe such thoughts and images, this section will help you.

The purpose of these next couple of exercises is twofold. First, becoming more aware of what is running through your mind will help you become more objective about your thoughts so that you no longer just accept them as facts. In other words, increasing your self-awareness can change your relationship with your thoughts. Second, an awareness of the thoughts and images that undermine your self-confidence will give you new material to explore later.

Exercise 36: Recognizing Thoughts and Images That Have Occupied Your Mind

First, think back to the exercises in chapters 7, 8, and 9. These involved mindfulness, further preparation for compassion, and developing the compassionate mind. As you did these exercises, were you aware of any thoughts or images (recurring or not) that popped into your mind and undermined your self-confidence? These thoughts or images may have related to events in the past, present, or future. If you are aware of any, make a note of them in your notebook or journal.

Now review all the notes you have been taking while working your way through this book. Can you identify any self-undermining thoughts or images that may have prevented you from building your self-confidence?

Finally, thinking back over the last week or month, can you recall any particular times when you felt as though your self-confidence was undermined? If you can, bring to mind a situation to which you feel comfortable returning. Imagine yourself back in that situation again for just a few moments. Close your eyes to help you reconnect with the experience. Now answer the following questions:

1.   What were you thinking of in general in that situation?

2.   What was the anxious part of your brain thinking…
       …about thoughts and images that relate to you, to other people, or to the world in general?

3. What was the sad part of your brain thinking...

   ...about thoughts and images that relate to you, to other people, or to the world in general?

4. What was the angry part of your brain thinking...

   ...about thoughts and images that relate to you, to other people, or to the world in general?

5. What was the envious part of your brain thinking...

   ...about thoughts and images that relate to you, to other people, or to the world in general?

6. What do you fear most about this situation?

7. Have you noticed any self-critical or undermining thoughts or images going through your mind during this exercise?

8. Are there any rules you are aware of that, in this situation, you are applying to yourself, to other people, or to the world in general?

Once you feel you have explored the situation sufficiently, engage in your soothing-rhythm breathing or your preferred imagery exercise to access your soothing system. (Returning your mind to a specific situation is difficult, so it may help to use your soothing-rhythm breathing, place-of-contentment, or compassion exercises at set intervals during the course of this exercise.)

Susan's worksheet shows what she discovered through this exercise.

Susan's Worksheet: Recognizing Undermining Thoughts and Images

1. Undermining thoughts or images that arose during exercises in chapters 7 to 9:

    I can't focus my mind. I'm useless at this.

    I don't deserve to feel compassionate about myself. Change isn't happening fast enough.

2. Undermining thoughts and images from journal:

    Images of my mom wagging her finger at me. I'm pathetic.

    I've got to get on and change things because I am wasting my life.

    I'll never get the hang of this.

3. Undermining thoughts or images in relation to boss recently criticizing work:

    I'm going to be found out as someone who can't do her job. I'm never going to feel any different.

    Doesn't she realize I am trying my hardest?

    It's not fair. Paula did something very similar and she gets away with everything.

    I'm going to lose this job. I'll never achieve anything.
    There's no point in trying so hard at work because my best isn't good enough.

More on Physiotherapy for the Brain

If you wanted to develop your biceps, simply raising your arms up and down from the elbow would be unlikely to have the desired effect. Neither would it be a good idea to try to lift a very heavy weight right away. To make the changes we need to make, sensibly and efficiently, the key is to work against a comfortable amount of resistance.

This is true for the work you are embarking on now. If the exercises were easy, it would indicate that this is not where you necessarily need to be directing your efforts. If, on the other hand, closing your eyes and engaging in these exercises for ten minutes is too hard for you and produces high levels of emotion, this also is an ineffective use of your time and effort. You need to work at an intensity that produces the best results for you, which is achievable but not too easy. Remember, whenever you feel overstretched, use a mindfulness or soothing exercise for a period of time until the emotions subside, just as you would take a break at the gym.

Exercise 37: Noticing Thoughts and Images as They Occur in Your Mind

To recognize thoughts and images that are occupying your mind and undermining your self-confidence, do the following two things.

1. Start to make notes relating to your practice of mindfulness or compassionate imagery in difficult situations over the coming week. After completing each exercise, jot down in your notebook or journal any undermining thoughts and images that came up.

2. Over the week ahead, identify and explore any situations where your self-confidence is undermined, and whenever this happens, warmly bring your attention to whatever thoughts and images are occupying your mind at the time. If identifying these situations is difficult to do, look out for variations in your emotions, physical sensations, or certain behaviors as markers, or prompts. For example, some people find that the first thing they notice is a sense of dread or anxiety, maybe anger. Others notice physical sensations such as a faster heart rate, sweating, a dry mouth, tension, or a sense of heaviness. Some people may

notice that they feel dirty or contaminated and have the urge to wash. Others note that they crave food, alcohol, or a cigarette when they know they don't need it or may start to pick at their skin or scratch.

All of these things should be viewed as prompts, reminding you to ask yourself, *What is running through my mind right now?* Engaging with your soothing-rhythm breathing at such times can help you warmly observe. You can then ask yourself the same questions that you asked in exercise 36, but switch to the present tense:

1. What are you thinking of in general in this situation?

2. What is the anxious part of your brain thinking…
    …about thoughts and images that relate to you, to other people, or to the world in general?

3. What is the sad part of your brain thinking…
    …about thoughts and images that relate to you, to other people, or to the world in general?

4. What is the angry part of your brain thinking…
    …about thoughts and images that relate to you, to other people, or to the world in general?

5. What is the envious part of your brain thinking…
    …about thoughts and images that relate to you, to other people, or to the world in general?

6. What do you fear most about this situation?

7. Have you noticed any self-critical or undermining thoughts or images going through your mind during this exercise?

8. Are there any rules you are aware of that, in this situation, you are applying to yourself, to other people, or to the world in general?

It may be helpful to have these questions written down in your notebook or journal and to have them ready for use whenever a difficult situation arises.

Reflection on Exercises 36 and 37

As you do these exercises, it can be tempting to try to work out what happened. If this occurs, just acknowledge that this is a common tendency and then return to becoming aware of thoughts and images with curiosity.

Whether you are reflecting on a difficult situation or in the middle of one, your soothing-rhythm breathing can bring your soothing system online and allow you space and time to think things through. That said, some people find self-soothing so effective that it turns off their thoughts and/or prevents them from being able to access them. Use the practice in whatever way is most helpful to you.

These exercises place an emphasis on noticing thoughts and images associated with specific situations, but many people find that their thoughts and images are not limited to the particular situation in progress. Thoughts and images from the past, as well as thoughts and predicted images of the future, may also occur.

In social situations, for example, David had thoughts such as *They think I am boring* or *I just can't click with people*, and this led to others, like *I'm never going to meet a partner*, and mental images of himself ten years older, still living in a flat on his own.

Valerie found that whenever she felt anxious in social situations, she not only had thoughts such as *I look really anxious* and *People are noticing I am anxious and are judging me*, but she also had a visual image of herself looking red and flustered, together with an image of herself in the playground at school, being taunted by other children.

Whether the thoughts and images that you notice are limited to the present situation or also include the past, the future, or both, the key is just to notice this and bring such thoughts into your awareness.

GENERATING COMPASSIONATE ALTERNATIVE THOUGHTS AND IMAGES

Once you have begun to notice the thoughts and images that are occupying your mind and undermining your self-confidence, generating compassionate alternatives may help your new brain to change this pattern for the better. Doing this can help you stand back from a situation and take a more rounded and realistic viewpoint. This way, it's less likely that you will be biased and emotionally controlled by the thoughts and images in your head. The following exercise will ask your new brain to respond to your old brain and, through this process, help you reach conclusions that reflect all of the brain's capacity rather than just one side of it.

A Question of Balance

Understandably you may wonder, *What if my old brain was right? What if people really are judging me negatively? What if I am about to lose my job? What if my partner is having an affair?*

Generating compassionate alternative thoughts isn't about overruling any instincts that you may have; it's about allowing yourself to look at the broader picture and to draw a more considered conclusion. If you then conclude that your initial instincts were right, your new brain can help you deal with this. It can give you the strength and courage to cope with difficult things. It can help you face any pain and upset and remind you of your own resilience. It can bring to mind other difficulties you have faced and coped with in the past. It can prepare you and coach you through the most trying situations.

By now, you are probably more aware of the range of thoughts and images that run through your mind in different situations. Now you are going to look specifically at those that undermine your self-confidence.

To generate compassionate alternative thoughts and experience their benefits, the compassionate-mind approach recommends the following five steps.[1]

Step 1 involves writing down difficult thoughts and images that you are having, or have become aware of, on a compassionate thoughts/images worksheet.

Step 2 involves engaging with the pragmatic part of your brain—the reporter rather than the interrogator—and using it to gain a more balanced perspective of the information at hand. It is not a matter of kidding yourself into new ways of thinking but of drawing conclusions that are considered and balanced. You can use the following questions to generate alternative viewpoints:

- *If I stood back from this situation, could there be another way of viewing it?*

- *Is there any evidence that would not support the conclusions I have drawn?*

- *If I weren't experiencing strong emotions, would I think any differently about the situation, about myself, or about other people?*

- *If I were looking back a year from now, would I view things in the same way?*

- *If a friend were thinking in this way, what would I say to him or her? What would I want a friend to say to me?*

- *What would someone who cared or cares about me say?*

- *Have there been occasions in the past when I have thought this way, but the conclusions I drew proved to be incorrect?*

- *Even if I am correct, are there things that I could say to myself that would be helpful?*

---

1   The term *experience* is used here to recognize that the aim of the exercise is to generate alternative thoughts but also to feel the effect of having such thoughts, therefore turning an intellectual exercise into an emotional one.

- *Am I expecting unrealistic things of the situation, other people, or myself?*

- *What may be or might have been going on for the other people involved?*

- *Is it more about other people or the situation than it is about me?*

Step 3 involves using your compassionate mindset to help generate a different, more compassionate perspective on your thoughts and images. This may be through using your ideal compassionate self, your perfect nurturer, or your compassionate coach—whatever you feel would be most helpful to you. The following questions may further guide your self-compassionate responses to distressing thoughts:

Has my compassionate mind responded sensitively and validated the reasons the situation and the emotions I experience may be difficult?

Do my responses…

…convey understanding, acceptance, and caring?

…recognize that we are a complex species, and this means that we often struggle?

…recognize that we are prone to self-criticism?

…remain nonjudgmental?

…reflect on whichever one of the three emotion regulation systems it would be helpful for me to focus upon at the moment?

…remind me that I am not on my own, for millions of people struggle to build their self-confidence?

…recognize that life can be hard and sometimes people can do things that hurt us?

…allow me to be moved by my experiences rather than avoid things?

Step 4 involves once again using your compassionate mind and, rereading what you have written on the worksheet, allowing each new conclusion to have more emotional impact. Remember, your compassionate mind has the ability to support you through difficult feelings and times. This can help turn something you know into something you feel.

Step 5 involves looking over what you have written and experienced and maybe finding ways to build further upon it. To help you review your worksheet, you can ask yourself the following questions:

- *Are the alternative thoughts and images that I have written down helpful to me?*

- *When I read what I have written (whether silently or out loud), is my tone of voice warm, soothing, and ultimately helpful?*

- *Can I evoke a sense of warmth when I read through the alternatives generated?*

Harry's story illustrates how taking these five steps can be a useful exercise.

• *Harry's Story*

Harry struggled with his self-confidence. This was largely due to difficulties he had had at school. Although naturally quite shy, Harry found himself in a group of very confident boys who came from quite affluent backgrounds. Harry's family, on the other hand, struggled to make ends meet. He wore hand-me-downs from his older brother and was unable to attend many school trips or after-school classes because they cost too much money.

When Harry was thirteen, his family moved farther away from school. Harry had fewer opportunities to see his friends and became more isolated. He felt angry that his friends made no effort to come see him; instead, they expected him to come to them. Harry decided to broach the subject, but instead of sorting things out, it led to a big argument, and afterward, his friendships never felt the same. Feeling low, Harry withdrew from his family, and feelings of inadequacy took over. He became anxious in a range of situations, especially in classes where his old friends were. Harry coped by constantly monitoring himself for signs that he might appear anxious. He also found that he became extremely careful about what he said to people; he was so fearful of rejection.

At the age of fifteen, when a boy his own age moved in next door and joined the school, life turned a corner. The two boys became friends, and in helping the new kid become familiar with the local area and school, Harry found he was able to rebuild some of his self-confidence. The preceding two years had taken their toll, however, and had left Harry with a tendency to feel anxious and inadequate.

As an adult, Harry found that in a range of stressful situations, his mind would become full of undermining thoughts. Although some were very specific to the situation he found himself in, he could identify key recurring themes. To generate compassionate alternative thoughts and imagery, Harry took the following five steps. First, he recorded his undermining thoughts and images (see the left-hand column of the following worksheet). Harry then asked himself some questions to generate alternative viewpoints (step 2). In the right-hand column of his worksheet, he recorded his rational alternative thoughts and images.

Step 3 involved Harry recruiting his compassionate mind to help him gain a more compassionate perspective on his situation. He chose to do this by first engaging in his soothing-rhythm breathing. After a few minutes, he then evoked the image of his ideal compassionate self and reminded himself of the key attributes and qualities of compassion, feeling them in his own mind and body. In this mindset, he examined each of his undermining thoughts and slowly responded to each situation compassionately.

Harry's Worksheet: Compassionate Alternative Thoughts and Images

Undermining Thoughts and Images	Alternative Thoughts and Images
I'm going to mess up.	*I never totally screw up. There are many times that I can recall where things have gone well. On the whole, I am doing okay.*
	Just because something isn't perfect, it doesn't mean I have messed up.
	My anxiety and threat system is talking. That's what it does; it is unlikely to be right.
	Even if I do mess things up I will learn from this and grow.
People are watching me and judging me negatively.	*People judge me less than I think they do; it's just my anxiety talking when I am in the middle of an anxiety-provoking situation.*
	Some people are willing me on to do well.
	I have had good feedback in the past: sometimes about me as a person or my work.
	In actual fact, it's hard to like someone who is perfect, so I shouldn't try to be.
	Julie often looks anxious in meetings, and I don't think any the worse of her. I actually think it's quite endearing.
	Tom always presents himself and his work really well, but I know he struggles in other areas.

I'm a waste of space.	I can't be that bad, as I have managed to remain in this job for over twelve months.
	There are aspects of myself that I am happy with.
	I have some good friends who seem to want to spend time with me.
	I have a range of positive qualities. I am a good listener. I can have a laugh.
I'm going to be alone.	No one can say for sure whether they are going to end up alone or not. All I can do is increase my chances of meeting someone and ensure I have some good friends around me.
Things always go wrong/images of key times when things have gone wrong.	There are times when things have gone right; they are just difficult to access when I am feeling low or anxious.
	I have been successful in a couple of interviews.
	I managed to rent a good flat.
	I have had some good nights out. I have some good friendships and enjoy a number of things.
Why do I do this to myself all the time? I am so annoying.	I continue to put myself forward for things because I want things to be better. I want to grow.
	We all have to start somewhere and I cannot expect myself never to make mistakes.
	It may be helpful to think of myself as being in training. By putting myself out there, be it in work or in relationships, I am being courageous, but there will be times when I am disappointed.

Harry chose to add each of his compassionate responses to the bottom of the worksheet. Alternatively, he could have chosen to link them specifically to each of the points in the first column, embedding them within the worksheet. His additional thoughts and images included the following:

- "Things are often difficult—life can be hard."

- "It is understandable that I feel as I do about things."

- "Some people do make judgments, and there are often things I cannot control—this can be difficult."

- "Such things don't happen only to me."

- "I have had a difficult time, and it is understandable that I still struggle with things."

- "Of course, I want things to be better, but it may be more helpful to support myself rather than undermine myself (retain image of the compassionate instead of the critical teacher, seeing myself walking toward the compassionate one and standing by her side)."

- "I am building my self-confidence, and it helps me to use my compassionate coach's strength and wisdom."

- "It helps to be understanding of my difficulties but also to learn from setbacks and use them to help me move forward."

Harry took a short break and then, in the penultimate step of this exercise (step 4), he once again evoked a compassionate mindset. He engaged in his soothing-rhythm breathing and then brought to mind his compassionate coach. In this frame of mind, Harry then slowly read though all of his compassionate alternative thoughts and images, allowing time for each of them to resonate with him. This helped the alternatives have more impact and reduced his old brain's capacity to dismiss them.

Finally, in step 5, Harry reviewed once more what he had written and experienced. He reflected that when he read aloud what he'd written, he did it in a warm and soothing tone, and the experience was truly helpful to him.

In time, Harry found that repeated use of this exercise made it easier for him to readily access such thoughts and associated feelings, not only while carrying out exercises to improve his self-confidence but also when he found himself in difficult situations.

Harry's story is a comprehensive example, designed to show an across-the-board approach to someone's problems. You may find it easier to choose one undermining thought or image at a time, working through it in isolation, rather than attempting to work through all of your problems at once.

Rather than continue to focus on thoughts and images that undermine your self-confidence, do the following exercise to help you generate compassionate thoughts. Remember, the emphasis is on finding something that works for you. Don't worry too much about getting the exercise right or about being neat or concise. Throw yourself into it and explore what is in your mind and what alternatives you can come up with.

Exercise 38: Giving Your New and Compassionate Brain a Voice

Use the following worksheet to record your compassionate thoughts and images, or write in your notebook or journal. Remember to take the following steps:

1. Notice and record any difficult thoughts and images.

2. Generate alternative thoughts and images.

3. Use a compassionate-mind exercise to generate a more compassionate perspective and add this to what you've already written.

4. While in your compassionate mindset, slowly read through the compassionate alternative thoughts and images you have come up with, allowing time for them to sink in and have an emotional impact on you.

5. Review what you have written.

To find assistance at these different stages, you can refer to the outline of the five steps that appeared earlier in this chapter. Specifically, it may help to ask yourself the questions that were listed under the descriptions of steps 2, 3, and 5.

Worksheet 7: Your Compassionate Alternative Thoughts and Images

Undermining Thoughts and Images	Alternative Thoughts and Images

Reflection on Exercise 38

Some people find that they can come up with alternative thoughts and images, be they pragmatic or compassionate, without the need to write things down, and at times this may be the only option. For example, it would be hard to write while driving, in the middle of a meeting, or on a night out. However, more often than not, committing thoughts to paper can help to focus the mind. While engaged in writing, people often find that they can keep their emotions in check and concentrate instead on working out the problem confronting them. I find that it's a bit like mental arithmetic: if I try to work things out in my mind, I get lost in all the ramifications. I also become easily distracted by what is going on around me. However, if I write things down, it's much easier for me to keep track of every aspect of the problem.

Step 5 of the process helps to highlight the things it may be beneficial for you to consider further. If you find, for example, that you experience doubts about certain alternative thoughts or images, evoke your compassionate mind once more and investigate matters further. Are there other things that you are telling yourself that may account for your feelings of doubt? Does the alternative perhaps arouse strong emotional responses in you? Is the critical part of yourself stepping in and again undermining things for you? Noticing sticking points can be really important, as this will guide you toward areas that still need to be addressed before you can build your self-confidence further.

Finally, you may find it helpful to write down key thoughts on the front or back cover of your notebook or on postcards to keep readily accessible. Brief statements that are personally significant, such as "It is understandable that sometimes I struggle," may suffice. You may prefer to write more comprehensive statements (or a combination of the two), such as "I have been through a lot...it takes time to build self-confidence. Each day, I will nurture myself and use my courage to grow. When I have setbacks, I will be both kind and encouraging to myself. I will then reflect and take a further step tomorrow." Before reading these statements, don't forget to use your soothing-rhythm breathing and to evoke a compassionate mindset. Being in a compassionate mindset will help these statements sink in.

CHAIR WORK

Having paid attention to the undermining or self-critical thoughts that run through your mind and then generated compassionate alternatives, you can now put to a different use the imagery work covered in chapters 7 through 9. In this section, you will learn how to use two chairs to help in addressing your self-undermining.

Chair work is used in a number of ways in psychological therapy. In this instance, you will use it to evoke different aspects of yourself, namely the part of you that may be struggling and your compassionate mindset (your ideal compassionate self, your perfect nurturer, or your compassionate coach or teacher). Because people prefer to use different imagery to evoke a compassionate mindset, this exercise will refer to the *compassionate role*. Chapter 9 looked at how using particular smells, textures, music, or pictures can help you to switch on your compassionate mindset. If you found this of help previously, it may be beneficial to use these prompts again during this exercise.

Exercise 39: Two Chairs

Begin by bringing to mind a situation where you have struggled, a time that evoked an emotional response in you. This may be a situation you have looked at in a previous exercise or one that you have written down in your notebook or journal. It will be something you are happy to work on now but which has previously made you feel anxious, low, or angry and has undermined your self-confidence.

Now place two chairs so that they are almost facing each other but at a slight angle, maybe as you would arrange the chairs together if a friend were visiting.

Now, sitting in one of the chairs, assume the role of the part of you that is struggling. Allow yourself to express your worries, concerns, and frustrations out loud. It may feel quite uncomfortable or unnatural doing this at first. Because the exercise is focusing on your thoughts, try to stay with these rather than get too deep into the associated emotions. Strong emotions can turn off the speech centers of the brain, and it is important that you get a conversation going here. Take time to voice everything that is troubling you.

Once you feel you have described the situation out loud, stand up and walk around for a while or sit quietly in a completely different chair. Practice your soothing-rhythm breathing. When you are ready, sit down in the second chair. Assume your compassionate posture with your spine strong but your body relaxed. Bring to mind the compassionate role that works best for you and experience the warmth that this evokes. As you engage your compassionate mind, imagine sitting in the presence of the part of you that is struggling; you may find that your facial expression softens. Remind yourself of the attributes and qualities of your compassionate role: tolerant of distress, warm and wise, nonjudgmental, and possessing great courage. Experience these qualities for a few moments in your mind and body.

Now, with warmth in your voice and heart, speak to the part of you that is struggling. Maybe acknowledge that you are experiencing difficulties and that life is hard for you. Acknowledge the fact that a whole range of factors has led to this difficult situation, and it is not your fault but a product of your biology and experiences. This might make you feel uncomfortable. If so, just allow yourself time to settle, maybe again engaging in your soothing-rhythm breathing. When you are ready, assume the role once more, just as an actor steps into the skin of someone he or she is attempting to portray.

Speaking out loud, address the struggling part of yourself. It may help to point out that many people struggle similarly and you are not alone in this. Perhaps remind yourself of other times when you have overcome setbacks and grown from them.

When you feel as though the compassionate role you have inhabited has voiced all it wishes to share, stand up once again. After spending a little time with your soothing-rhythm breathing, return to the first chair. Settle yourself for a moment. Now imagine yourself back into the first role, sitting in the presence of your compassionate self and hearing what it has to say, feeling its warmth toward you. Sit still and experience this sensation for a while.

Only when you feel that you have gotten as much as you can from this exercise, and while keeping hold of the emotions it has evoked in you, pick up your notebook or journal and jot down some reminders for yourself. Ask yourself such questions as *What did the compassionate self say or want me to know? How did it perceive me, this situation, and others like it?*

Once you feel you have recorded all the important points, stand up and walk around for a while. If this is difficult, you may choose to sit in a different chair altogether. Engage with your soothing-rhythm breathing. When you are ready, sit down in the compassionate chair once more. Is there anything else you should add to your summary, other things you would like to say to the part of you that is struggling?

Finally, slowly read through the points that you have recorded. Allow yourself the time to experience the words and feel them emotionally.

Reflection on Exercise 39

When faced with this exercise, some people find a number of reasons not to do it. They fear they will find it uncomfortable and, understandably, want to avoid this. But my advice is always "What have you got to lose?" You don't need to do this in the presence of others; you can do it in the privacy of your own home. Time and time again, people go on to report that, despite their initial reservations, having given it a go, they found it to be one of the most powerful exercises they've tried.

Some report finding no reason to speak while in the compassionate role. Others tell me that they direct warmth or colors toward the self that is struggling, or they direct gentle waves of soothing energy. Having returned to the original chair, they then find that this has helped. Some people seem to need a different way of viewing their situations before they can bring about an emotional change in themselves, whereas others find that they can experience such changes without the need for this sort of role-playing. Of course, as ever, the key is finding something that works for you. However, I would always suggest trying to give the compassionate role a voice, for it can be very effective.

CONCLUSIONS

It is apparent that the thoughts and images that occupy our minds can play a key role in undermining our self-confidence. They can also help us to build it when combined with a compassionate frame of mind. The next chapter will look at compassionate letter writing as a means of further building your self-confidence.

11

Compassionate
Letter Writing

The art of writing is the art of discovering what you believe.

—Gustave Flaubert

In this chapter you will learn how to use compassionate letter writing as a way of further exploring your capacity for inner support and self-compassion. Compassionate letter writing can also help you generate new ways of thinking and, at times, generate ideas about things it may be helpful for you to address. This in turn can help you build your self-confidence.

After reading the guidelines below, you will be asked to write three specific letters. These will be

1. a compassionate letter to yourself specifically focused on building your self-confidence,

2. a compassionate letter to yourself from the perspective of your ideal compassionate self or compassionate role (such as

a compassionate teacher, coach or companion, or your perfect nurturer), and

3. a compassionate letter to yourself that focuses on worksheet 7, where you recorded some compassionate alternative thoughts and images.

GUIDELINES FOR COMPASSIONATE LETTER WRITING

Before you begin, here are some tips for how to get the most out of compassionate letter writing.

Take Time to Experience What You Are Writing

During these exercises, you will be asked to engage both the intellectual and the emotional part of your brain, so take your time and allow yourself to feel each sentence, phrase, or word you use.

Take a Break Whenever It Is Helpful

Some people find it difficult to concentrate on letter writing and become frustrated by this. Others find that focusing their efforts on certain things can evoke strong physical sensations: for example, a sense of numbness or difficult emotions, such as sorrow, anger, or anxiety. Although at times it is helpful to stay with these difficult experiences, at others it may be preferable to take a break. At such times, it may help to evoke your compassionate mind via an imagery exercise or by using your soothing-rhythm breathing. It may also help to get up and move around for a time. Then, when you are ready, return to the exercise once more.

Alternatively, it may help to focus your letter on the difficulty at hand. For example, you could write: "As I sit here and write this letter, it is understandable that I feel strong emotions because..." Or, from a different perspective, you may write: "I am sorry that writing this letter is painful for you and evokes difficult emotions. I can understand why this would be....You are courageous to embark on this work."

Remember That Your Letter Does Not Have to Be Perfect

Don't worry about your handwriting, spelling, or grammar. You may prefer to write in sentences and paragraphs. Alternatively, it may be helpful to build pauses into compassionate letters by the use of multiple ellipses. For some people, this helps slow down the train of thought. For example, in part of the letter you may write something like this: "It is not your fault......stand tall......breathe......you are not alone...... others struggle......connect."

Try not to let perfectionism and self-criticism cause you to over-think your letters. Remember, the aim is to call upon self-compassion and inner support, not to achieve an A.

My Personal Story about Writing

At school, I managed to develop a style of handwriting that I thought covered up my poor spelling, and it worked for a while. By the time I got to secondary school, my difficulties with word blindness and spelling were identified. This was a mixed blessing. Suddenly, I had people to help me. Unfortunately, however, this was often done in a shaming way with a thick red marker pen and extra lessons before school every day. My poor handwriting was also picked up on, which, by now, was very difficult to correct. For both of these reasons, writing can be associated with difficult emotions for me, but when I do these exercises, it helps to reflect that my ideal compassionate self or compassionate coach is supportive of my efforts and me. It's not concerned about my handwriting, grammar, or spelling. Instead, it's concerned about the way I feel about myself.

Remember That Letters Can Be Long or Short

In some cases, it takes only a few words to access inner support and self-compassion, whereas sometimes more detail is required to get to the same place. It's not how much you write but how it makes you feel.

If It Helps, Build Upon the Work of Others

You will find several short examples of compassionate letters in this chapter, and further examples can be found on the Compassionate Mind website (www.compassionatemind.co.uk). It may help you to look at some of these before writing one to yourself.

Combine the Practice with Other Things You Have Found Useful

If you have found that a particular smell, texture, picture, or color has helped you to access your compassionate mind more readily, it may help to use such prompts during this exercise also.

Start When Things Are Relatively Easy

As with any of the exercises in this book, it is best to embark on the process of compassionate letter writing when you are feeling relatively stable emotionally rather than when you are facing problems. As you become more familiar with the practice, you can then use it at more difficult times.

Use Simple Letter-Writing Materials

All you need is your notebook, journal, or a sheet of paper, along with a pen or pencil. It may be helpful to have your notes and summary sheets from previous exercises to remind yourself of work you have done.

GUIDING PRINCIPLES FOR COMPASSIONATE LETTERS

The following principles may be useful whenever you write a compassionate letter to yourself:

Be sensitive to and validate the emotions you experience.

Convey understanding, acceptance, and caring.

Validate the reasons you may be struggling with certain things.

Recognize that human beings are a complex species, and this means we often struggle.

Recognize that we are all prone to self-criticism, and although your self-critic has your best intentions at heart, listening to it is not the best way to build self-confidence.

Remain nonjudgmental.

Reflect on which of the emotion regulation systems it would be helpful for you to work on at the moment (see diagram 1 in chapter 2).

Remind yourself that you are not on your own. Millions of other people struggle to build their self-confidence.

Recognize that life can be hard, and sometimes other people can do things that hurt us.

Rather than avoid difficult situations, allow yourself to be moved by your own experiences.

These principles also may be useful in reviewing a compassionate letter after you've finished writing it.

COMPASSIONATE LETTER-WRITING PRACTICES

As the aim of this book is to build your self-confidence, the first letter-writing exercise will focus on writing a letter to help build your self-confidence. Because this is likely to be your first experience of compassionate letter writing, the exercise provides a template to guide you.

This exercise will be followed by some variations and adaptations for you to try. Hopefully, some form of letter writing will become an integral part of your ongoing self-confidence building. After you've carried out each exercise, you may want to write down a few notes or reflections on your personal practice summary sheet or in your notebook or journal.

While posture is an important factor in all exercises, in letter writing it is particularly important. You will be asked to adopt a self-confident posture like the posture you have found useful before, one with alertness and strength in it, paired with warmth and openness. Given that you will be writing, it may be helpful to raise your chin slightly higher or imagine a core of strength running through your body. Alternatively, you may become aware of a sense of strength in your chest, as you experience an expansion in this area of the body.

This first exercise will encourage you to come up with some ideas for things you can do to help build your self-confidence. You may be able to use these ideas in chapter 12, which focuses on taking action.

Exercise 40: Compassionate Letter Writing to Build Your Self-Confidence

Begin by spending a little time refamiliarizing yourself with your compassionate formulation from chapter 4 (see diagram 4). This formulation drew together your influences and experiences, concerns and fears, and the coping strategies you've been using and their unintended drawbacks.

Now, find a place that is, as far as possible, free from distractions, somewhere you can be for an hour or so. If this seems too daunting, start by aiming to work on this exercise for just ten to fifteen minutes. Feel strength and alertness in your spine, with a relaxed and open posture.

If it is helpful to you, start by using your soothing-rhythm breathing or place-of-contentment exercise. Now use one of the imagery exercises outlined in chapter 9 to evoke a compassionate mindset. Alternatively you can use one of the mindfulness practices described in chapter 7 to create a sense of calm awareness, or else simply go straight into the exercise once your mind and body are settled.

Remind yourself of the compassionate attributes and qualities, such as warmth, nonjudgment, empathy, wisdom, and strength, feeling them in your mind and body. Feel a gentle smile on your face and adjust your posture to embody a sense of strength and self-confidence.

Use the template in the following worksheet to guide you in your letter writing, filling in the blanks following each statement.

Worksheet 8: A Template for Compassionate Letter Writing

It is understandable that I have found it difficult to build my self-confidence because...

_____

_____

_____

(Tip: Include both past experiences and current circumstances. Gently, with warmth, attempt to convey empathy and understanding in what you write.)

It is understandable that I have developed concerns and fears about...

_____

_____

_____

I have coped by...

_____

_____

_____

But there have been unintended consequences and drawbacks, such as...

_____

_____

_____

One of the unintended consequences is that my self-confidence has not developed. This is not my fault, but it is my responsibility to change my future.

(Tip: Don't forget, as you are writing, to retain your self-confident posture with your chin up and a feeling of strength in the chest.)

Now I am committing myself to building my self-confidence, but this will take time. I recognize that I have the capacity for strength, courage, resilience, and wisdom.

(Now imagine yourself being in the presence of your compassionate coach.)

My compassionate coach would remind me that...

_____

_____

_____

I have already taken a number of steps toward building my self-confidence. These include...

_____

_____

_____

In the past, when I was struggling with difficult situations, it would have helped me if those around me had been more nurturing of my self-confidence and...

_____

_____

_____

At the time, it would have also helped me if I had done the following things to nurture myself and build my self-confidence...

_____

_____

_____

With this in mind, it may be helpful for me now to...

_____

_____

_____

(Tip: Avoid *shoulds* and *musts*. And, remember, the idea is to be encouraging and nurturing. Therefore, big goals can be broken down into small and manageable steps.)

If I had setbacks, my compassionate coach would remind me that...

_____

_____

_____

The emotions my compassionate coach would direct my way would be...

_____

_____

_____

When you feel you have written enough, put down your pen and center yourself by doing one of the exercises you have found helpful, such as your soothing-rhythm breathing or visiting your place of contentment. Finally, slowly read through your letter, with a feeling of warmth and strength toward yourself, and allow the words to sink in.

• *Andy's Story Continued*

You may remember Andy from chapter 4. His difficulties with self-confidence had partly arisen from his family's overprotectiveness toward him during a long childhood illness. In his teens and later at college, Andy had always felt socially isolated by his inability to be able to join his friends in sports activities.

Andy charted his experiences and feelings in his formulation (diagram 3). He later revisited this formulation when he chose to write a compassionate letter to himself. He used the template in worksheet 8 as a guide, but he focused on the parts that were most relevant to him and changed some of the wording where appropriate. Here is his letter:

It is understandable that I have found it difficult to build my self-confidence. I have been through a lot, with my physical health problems and having very confident siblings, to problems fitting in with my sporty friends and using alcohol as a crutch. Given these things, it would be unusual for someone not to be concerned about his or her physical health. I can understand why I often feel different and am therefore susceptible to feelings of social isolation. I have developed a sense of being an outsider because I have had these early experiences.

I have coped by doing all manner of things, from beating myself up to drinking and avoidance tactics. But these strategies have drawbacks that prevent me from building my self-confidence.

This is not my fault, but it is my responsibility to change my future. Now I am committing time and effort to building my self-confidence. I recognize that I have the capacity for strength, courage, resilience, and wisdom, and my compassionate coach reminds me of these things. He also reminds me that he has my back and that, despite setbacks, with concerted efforts I can change things for the better.

I have already made a lot of progress. I have recognized this is an issue for me and bought this book. I have worked through the exercises so far, despite some difficulties and reservations.

I can't blame other people for my situation, as I never let them know I was struggling. If I had, they could have encouraged and supported me. I am going to do this for myself, but I am going to let certain people know what I am doing so I can gain their support.

I know I will have setbacks, but at such times, I will remind myself of the compassionate qualities and use the exercises in this book to practice self-compassion. I will grow and learn from each of my setbacks, recognizing that it is understandable for me to feel undermined by them, by looking at setbacks as an opportunity to learn more about myself.

Reflection on Exercise 40

If you find that the concept of a compassionate coach is not helpful to you, you may prefer to use the ideal compassionate self, compassionate companion or teacher, or the perfect nurturer.

Although some find it helpful to use the statements that are provided in the exercise template, other people find it restricting. You can adapt the wording to make it meaningful to your situation. Hopefully, you can see the general direction of the statements provided and then work out how to write it in your own words.

If you have found adopting a particular posture helpful, it may be useful to use this posture in all future exercises, not just while letter writing.

You can adapt this exercise to make it part of your regular self-practice; rather than consider your situation in general terms, you would think about the last twenty-four hours or the last week. An example of such a letter can be found in Jenny's story.

• *Jenny's Story*

Jenny worked at the local supermarket. She had passed by job promotions time and time again, saying to her employers that she was happy for the time being with her present role. Beneath the surface, the idea of a promotion filled her with dread. She feared she wouldn't be able to do the things required of her and would do a bad job. Gradually, as Jenny developed her self-confidence, she took on a few more new opportunities at work. Then, when her supervisor was taken ill, she was asked to take her role temporarily.

Jenny surprised herself by agreeing and felt proud both about being asked and about accepting the position. Although at certain times she felt overwhelmed, her new role was really rewarding. However, when another coworker went on sick leave, Jenny's workload suddenly increased. Over the course of a week, she found she had made a few silly errors, ones she never would have made previously. Jenny felt waves of anxiety. To address the return of her self-criticism over the remainder of the week, she was able to use compassionate imagery and soothing-rhythm breathing.

That weekend, Jenny recalled the mistakes she had made, and once again she felt a wave of anxiety. On noting this, she went to her room and, sitting quietly, engaged in her soothing-rhythm breathing. She then opened her journal and wrote:

It is understandable that I have found it difficult to build my self-confidence this week because there have been a whole number of new things happening at work, I have been pushed into new roles, and such things have activated my fears of failing. This was really tough.

In the past, I have coped by trying to get out of things, taking time off, or even taking beta-blockers, but all of these things prevented me from building my self-confidence. But recently, I decided to give things a shot, despite my concerns. This took a lot of guts, and I am glad I did it, despite finding it difficult. I used imagery exercises to help me accept the fact that I was anxious, and this also helped me believe that the mistakes I made did not mean that I was useless. I even told a couple of people that I felt anxious, and amazingly this really helped, as I felt supported by them.

Now, standing back from things, I can see that my self-confidence has actually grown this week. Maybe the best weeks for learning are the ones I also find difficult. In the future, it would help if I did what I did today. It would also help if I reminded myself that there was a positive outcome this week.

Exercise 41: Compassionate Letter Writing from the Compassionate Role to Yourself

Prepare for this exercise in the way you have previously found most helpful.

Now put pen to paper and write a supportive letter to yourself from the perspective of a compassionate role. Your letter could be focused on something very specific, such as how you are feeling right now or a situation that recently happened. Alternatively, it could take a more general stance with respect to how you view yourself. It may open with a statement like the following: "I am sorry that you are having a difficult time at the moment and are struggling to build your self-confidence." When you feel that you have completed your letter, put down your pen or pencil and for a few moments engage in one of the exercises aimed at evoking a compassionate frame of mind.

Now, when you feel ready, slowly reread your letter. Engage with the emotion that the letter conveys rather than focusing on how you have written it, the grammar, words, or phrasing.

Once you have done this, allow yourself to sit for a while, feeling a sense of warmth and allowing the exercise to sink in.

• *Tracy's Story*

Tracy's family was often critical of her. At a family gathering, she had watched as her uncle poked fun at her nephew Ben. Her nephew clearly looked upset. After taking a calming breath, Tracy remarked, "Don't be cruel, Paul." But instead of having the desired effect, her comment was met by a barrage of criticism. Tracy turned around and walked away, taking her nephew with her.

That evening, Tracy wrote the following compassionate letter to herself:

I am sorry that today has been really difficult for you. Being around certain people can be tough. It is understandable that you feel a whole range of emotions, such as frustration, anger, anxiety, and sadness, given what happened. This is a difficult environment in which to build your self-confidence.

But it would be helpful for you to acknowledge that you did volunteer your opinion and that this took courage. People are complicated, and sometimes it is helpful just to acknowledge that. Maybe they don't see what an impact this is having on you. Together we will build your self-confidence; I have your back through good times and setbacks. Each day you find out more about yourself and this will help you grow.

Reflection on Exercise 41

You may have noticed that when you are writing letters, referring to yourself in either the first person as "I" or in the second person as "you" works better. Some people, however, find that it makes no difference. It may be helpful to you to experiment further with these options and see which helps you best in different situations.

Exercise 42: Writing a Compassionate Letter Based on Compassionate Alternative Thoughts and Images

In this exercise, you will use your compassionate alternative thoughts and images from worksheet 7 as a focus. As you write a compassionate letter based on this worksheet, you may decide to focus on a thought or image that is associated with strong emotions. Alternatively, you may decide to start with one that is less challenging. The choice is yours.

First, familiarize yourself again with worksheet 7 and have it close at hand. You can prepare for this exercise in whatever manner you have found helpful with other exercises.

Now review your worksheet. To begin with, focus on the column containing your undermining thoughts and images and begin to write compassionately about such things. Hopefully, this part of the letter will be sensitive to your difficulties and validate the associated emotions.

When you feel that you have focused on the first column long enough, allow yourself time to review what you have written so far and let it sink in.

Now turn your attention to the second column of compassionate alternative thoughts and images. If you like, in your letter, expand on what you have written previously, in a way that the worksheet maybe did not allow space for.

Take time to explore in your letter all the work you did on the worksheet. When you feel as though your letter is complete, put your pen down for a few moments and engage once more in one of the centering exercises that you find helpful. This may be a mindfulness exercise, soothing-rhythm breathing, or some form of imagery.

After a short while, reread your letter slowly. You may prefer to read it out loud or in your head.

Once you have done this sit for a while, feeling a sense of warmth and allowing the exercise to sink in.

• *Alan's Story*

Upon arriving at work one day, Alan was met by his boss, who asked him to present some information at a meeting later that afternoon. This was something he had never done before, and Alan felt overwhelmed. During the day, he found time to record some compassionate alternative thoughts and images, and that evening he wrote a letter to himself based on what he'd recorded earlier.

First, he focused on writing compassionately about his undermining thoughts and images:

I am sorry that you often feel that you can't cope in situations. When you were put on the spot at work, it is understandable that you panicked. This then led you to feel upset and self-critical. You often tell yourself you are pathetic in these situations, and this goes back to school days when you were bullied.

Alan went on to write about his compassionate alternative thoughts and images:

It may be helpful to remind myself that I never totally screw up. In addition, I have a tendency to focus on the negative (like everyone else does to some extent), and as I recall, there were things that went well, such as...

Because of the experiences I have had, I have learned to be critical of myself, but I am now learning that it is more helpful to be self-compassionate and nurture myself...My compassionate coach knows that I am doing my best...I am doing my best...I am a human being who struggles. Many other people also struggle. It's not just me.

Reflection on Exercise 42

This specific letter-writing exercise is meant to help consolidate the work you have already begun with compassionate alternative thoughts and images. You may now decide to focus on other worksheets you have completed and perhaps regularly write a letter every time you complete a new one. You may find it beneficial to write down some compassionate alternative thoughts whenever events trigger strong emotions or feelings of self-criticism. In other words, you can use worksheet 7 in a reactive way. Later, you may choose to proactively write a compassionate letter to yourself, perhaps using a recent worksheet as the basis for it.

REVIEWING YOUR COMPASSIONATE LETTERS

Once you have completed a letter, it's a good idea to review it using the guiding principles found in this chapter. This can help to enhance your letter and its focus. Do this in a frame of mind that holds curiosity and warmth rather than one that is judgmental and cold.

As a starting point, you can take each of the guiding principles found earlier in this chapter and turn it into a question. For example, was your letter sensitive to and did it validate the emotions you experienced? Did it convey understanding, acceptance, and caring? Did it validate the reasons you may be struggling with certain things?

Second, does your letter capture a sense of warmth throughout? If you noticed that parts of it contain less warmth or are cold or even hostile, it may be worth warmly reflecting on why this may be. For example:

Did your self-critic step in?

Did you feel as though you were kidding yourself? Were you undermining your own efforts?

Was your drive or threat system kicking in, making such statements as *you should do X* and *you shouldn't do Y*?

All such observations are very helpful, as they direct us toward further avenues of exploration. Depending on the particular obstacle you notice, it may help to engage in an imagery exercise focusing on this difficulty or to complete a worksheet with compassionate alternative thoughts and images.

As a further exercise, many people find it helpful to write a letter looking specifically at the obstacle itself. Here's an example:

At times when I write in this way, I start telling myself I need to "get a grip." I get frustrated with myself and think the struggling part of me is pathetic. Reflecting upon where this comes from, I know that this is related to how I was treated in the past and that I have learned to do it to myself. It may be helpful for me to recall the story about which teacher I would send my child to. Of course I would choose the compassionate teacher, and this is the teacher it would be helpful for me to approach too, instead of the critical one. Through being compassionate to myself, I will gain strength and courage and reduce my tendency to judge myself.

ADAPTATIONS TO COMPASSIONATE LETTER WRITING

Here are some of the many ways people have used compassionate letter writing and enhanced their experience. It may be worth trying some of the following:

- Write different parts of your letter in different colored pens to emphasize different points.

- Record your letters, remembering to use a warm compassionate tone, and then play them back at different times when you are in need of compassion, maybe at the beginning or end of the day.

- Read a letter aloud to yourself in front of a mirror, again remembering to use a warm, compassionate tone.

- Read a letter while focusing on a photograph of yourself. Depending upon what the letter is about, it may help you to use a photograph of yourself as a child or as an adult. Sometimes holding a photo of yourself taken at a particular time, maybe when things were most difficult for you, can have a powerful effect.

- Add pictures, photographs, and drawings to your letters to increase their emotional impact.

- Write out complete letters or parts of longer letters on the back of postcards that you've chosen to convey a sense of warmth and carry them with you.

- Scent your letters with something that evokes a sense of warmth and is soothing. This may be a perfume, aftershave, or aromatherapy oil. Enjoy discovering a scent that is helpful for you.

- Use a specific chair that helps you evoke your compassionate mind and write while sitting in this chair.

- Sit in a chair and allow yourself to get in touch with difficult feelings surrounding a situation (past, present, or future). Once you have experienced and written about these feelings, move to a second chair, allowing yourself to step outside the previous feelings and to reflect on them, and then write from your new perspective.

- Sit in a chair and evoke your ideal compassionate self or compassionate image, such as your compassionate coach or companion. Remind yourself of all of its qualities and attributes. Now, facing a second chair, read out one of your letters. Then move to the second chair and experience what was said.

- Read your letters at different times of the day and before or after certain events to see if this is helpful to you.

- Look out for positive things (such as events, things people have said, how people have behaved, or things you have realized) during the day and make a note of them so you can use this as material for your next letter.

- Write a letter to your inner self-critic, acknowledging that it may have your welfare at heart but explaining how it's going about things the wrong way. Explain what you need to build your self-confidence.

- Write a letter to people in the past who might have hurt you, on purpose or not, telling them how you felt then and how you feel now. This can be an emotional exercise, so remember to evoke inner strength, support, wisdom, and courage from an imagery or breathing exercise.

- Write a letter to yourself as a younger person. What messages and emotions does your compassionate mind want the child or the younger adult to hear and feel?

- Write a letter to yourself from an older, wiser, compassionate you. What would you say to yourself now, and what would a compassionate future look like?

CONCLUSIONS

Compassionate letter writing can be an extremely powerful, emotional, and beneficial exercise. As you can see, there are a number of ways that you can adapt it or combine it with other ideas. Be creative and develop something that works for you.

Initially, it may be beneficial to engage in letter writing, as well as rereading letters, every week or even every day. Later it may be helpful to develop this into something that becomes an integral part of your life.

The next chapter will draw upon some of the ideas generated in your compassionate letters. These ideas will provide the focus for some new exercises aimed at taking action to increase compassionate behavior.

12

Taking Action with Compassionate Behavior

Courage is not the absence of fear, but rather the judgment that
something else is more important than fear.

—Ambrose Redmoon

It is worth reflecting that all the work you have done so far, from initially picking up this book to reading it, engaging in exercises, and
developing your own practices, is, in fact, self-compassionate behavior.
This chapter will focus on how you can take action to build your self-
confidence further by:

- Generating your own personal goals

- Identifying the steps you need to take

- Preparing to take action by using compassionate imagery,
  compassionate letter writing, coming up with compassionate

alternative thoughts and images, and preparing for compassionate behavioral experiments

- Taking action

- Reviewing your compassionate behavioral experiments and learning from them

Each of the exercises covered in this chapter is listed on your personal practice summary sheet in the preface. It may be helpful to use this sheet, as well as your journal or notebook, to record your reflections on these exercises.

GENERATING PERSONAL GOALS AND BREAKING THEM DOWN INTO MANAGEABLE STEPS

Building on all your previous work, it is important to focus on generating your goals from a compassionate mindset. In other words, you should warmly choose to work toward things that will benefit you. This is in contrast to responding to self-criticism (or the criticism of others) by deciding on things because you *should* or *have to* do them.

Here are some goals that other people wanting to build their self-confidence have worked toward:

- Meeting new people

- Public speaking

- Being comfortable handing in pieces of work that are not perfect

- Being able to put your point of view across to others

- Putting yourself forward for job opportunities

- Doing things just for pleasure

- Being able to ask for help

- Being able to apologize

- Stopping needless apologizing

- Being able to assert yourself in difficult relationships

- Being able to tell people how you feel

- Being able to return faulty goods or things you decide you don't want

- Saying no to people

- Saying yes to people

As you can see, there are many different things that you could focus on.

Exercise 43: Identifying Your Personal Goals Toward Building Your Self-Confidence

Find a place where you can be, as far as possible, free from major distractions for ten to fifteen minutes. Sit in a relaxed, open posture that has strength or alertness in it. Close your eyes or settle your gaze on a low fixed point.

Engage in your soothing-rhythm breathing or use your place-of-contentment imagery and experience a sense of soothing. Engage with this for a minute or so. Now bring to mind your compassionate coach, teacher, companion, or nurturer. Alternatively, evoke the sense of your ideal compassionate self. Remind yourself of the key compassionate qualities. Feel a sense of strength, courage, and warmth and allow a slight smile to appear on your face.

Now, in this frame of mind, ask yourself what goals it would be helpful for you to work toward: goals that will help you build your self-confidence.

If it is difficult for you to generate these goals, it may be worth reflecting on times in the past when you have lacked self-confidence. What was the situation, what happened, and what would you have done differently if you had been more self-confident? What would you change about yourself in the situation?

When you are ready, use the following worksheet to write down some specific goals that you wish to work toward. Then rate the goals from hardest to easiest by putting the number 1 by the goal that you think will be the most difficult, the number 2 by the goal you think is slightly less difficult, and so forth until you have rated all of them based on their difficulty to achieve.

Worksheet 9: Your Personal Goals

Your Goals	Difficulty Rating

Additional Hints for Generating Your Personal Goals

Your formulation from chapter 4 (see diagram 4) will probably give you some ideas for what you wish to work toward. For example, you may have identified a number of coping strategies that have unintended consequences or drawbacks. When Andy reviewed his formulation (see diagram 3), he was able to generate a number of additional goals, such as opening up to others, engaging in social activities he usually ignored, and reducing how much alcohol he drank.

You may find it helpful to ask someone you trust, someone who has your best interests at heart, for his or her thoughts. Further ideas could be drawn from the exercises you have done previously and your personal notes and reflections. It may be helpful to review these.

Exercise 44: Identifying the Steps You Need to Take

Starting with the goal you have identified as the least difficult in exercise 43, identify some simple steps that will help you achieve it. By doing so, you will break down the task into manageable stages, which will make it seem less overwhelming.

Once again, it will be helpful to adopt a compassionate mindset when approaching this exercise. Before beginning, you can skip ahead to James's story to see how this exercise worked for him. You can then return to the task of identifying the steps that you need to take.

Of course, if you feel ready to tackle your least difficult goal without breaking it down into smaller steps, go ahead and do so. Identifying the steps will be useful when you deal with more challenging goals.

Use the following worksheet to record the goal that you want to achieve and the steps that you will need to take to complete it. If necessary, you can use your journal or notebook to describe additional steps.

Worksheet 10: Steps to Completing Your Goal

Your goal:_____

Step 1:_____

Step 2:_____

Step 3: _____

Step 4:_____

Step 5: _____

Step 6:_____

• *James's Story*

James was twenty-four. Two years earlier he'd gotten his dream job of working at an entry level in a busy law firm. His self-confidence was low, but he knew that if he wished to progress in his chosen career, he would have to address this. Although James felt self-confident with his friends and family, his confidence often failed him at work and with strangers. He listed his six goals and then rated them on a scale of 1 to 6, from most difficult to easiest to achieve.

Goals	Difficulty Rating
Being able to contribute ideas at work	*3*
Getting on a busy underground train	*2*
Putting myself forward for the next round of promotions	*1*

Taking on a protégé at work	4
Being able to ask a stranger for directions	6
Taking something back to a shop	5

As you can see, James identified "being able to ask a stranger for directions" as the easiest goal for him to achieve. This goal was important to him, as he often had to make deliveries on foot to other law firms. The thought of asking someone for directions filled him with dread. All sorts of undermining thoughts would run through his head, such as They will think I am an idiot. They will see I am anxious. Or he would think, If I can't get this simple thing right, I am pathetic.

With the help of one of his close friends, James generated the steps he would need to take to accomplish his goal. Each step was designed to help him advance further toward achieving it.

Goal: *Being able to ask a stranger for directions*
Step 1: *Walk to the local main street at a quiet time and ask someone who seems approachable where the nearest pharmacy is, where a particular road is, or where the station is. Do this with three different strangers.*
Step 2: *Go into a busy street and ask someone who seems approachable where the nearest pharmacy is, where a particular road is, or where the station is. Do this with three different strangers.*
Step 3: *Repeat step 2 at rush hour.*
Step 4: *Repeat steps 2 and 3, but this time approach someone who looks busy or unapproachable.*
Step 5: *While making a work delivery to a known destination, ask a stranger if I am going to the right place. Do this with three different people.*
Step 6: *Next time I am making a delivery at work and need directions, ask a stranger for them.*

Reflection on Exercises 43 and 44

You can plan as many goals and associated steps as you want, and, of course, your plans are not set in stone. Many people modify the number of steps as they become more familiar with the process.

You may have been able to do these exercises very quickly, or you may need to think them through and add to them over a few days. What is important is that you proceed to the next exercise only when you feel ready.

Some people are daunted by their list of goals, while others find that they avoid writing down certain steps or goals because they think they are far too difficult or are associated with strong emotions. Remember, you are aiming to build your self-confidence step-by-step. You can proceed at your own pace, starting with your easiest goal and gradually taking on harder challenges.

PREPARING TO TAKE ACTION

This section outlines a range of different ways you can further prepare yourself to take action to build your self-confidence in both social and nonsocial situations. The next exercise is designed to prepare you specifically for building self-confidence in situations that involve other people.

When we are lacking in self-confidence, we can fall into a number of traps that stop us from thinking about a situation as a whole. For example, many people report that in social situations they feel as though they are being singled out in some way as if everyone were looking at them. Others view themselves totally through the eyes of other people. When we are lacking in self-confidence, we often believe we are acting in an unacceptable or disappointing way and that other people are scrutinizing and appraising us negatively.

You may already be aware of an imagery strategy that you can use to reduce your anxiety in such situations. For example, you can imagine interviewers or audience members in their underwear or perhaps sitting on the toilet. This strategy is aimed at bringing everyone to the same level and can help in situations where you feel intimidated, scrutinized, and judged.

This next exercise will ask you to use compassionate imagery to help change your perspective on a social situation.

Exercise 45: Using Compassionate Imagery to Prepare for Social Situations

Prepare for this exercise in the manner you have found most helpful previously. When you are ready, bring to mind a compassionate image (your perfect nurturer or compassionate coach or companion) or evoke the sense of your ideal compassionate self. Remind yourself of the key compassionate qualities. Feel a sense of strength and warmth, and allow a slight smile to appear on your face.

Now imagine the social situation you are preparing for. Imagine yourself in the situation. If you are imagining yourself as your ideal compassionate self, see the situation from this new perspective. Or imagine that your compassionate coach or companion or your perfect nurturer is supporting you in this situation. Draw a sense of strength and courage from this image.

Now turn your attention to each of the other people in the scene. Ask yourself what each one is likely to be experiencing. What are these people thinking? Attempt to take a comprehensive and compassionate view of their feelings.

If you notice that your threat system is activated, and you start to feel strong emotions, such as anxiety or anger, return to the soothing-rhythm breathing or imagery exercise you did in preparation. Remind yourself of the key compassionate qualities of strength, courage, and wisdom. When you are ready, resume the exercise.

When you feel you have explored this situation as well as you can, gently let the image fade and return to the image of your perfect nurturer, your compassionate coach or companion, or your ideal compassionate self. Engage in your soothing-rhythm breathing again if this is helpful.

After a few minutes, gently bring your awareness to the end of the exercise and become more aware of your physical environment.

•   *James's Story Continued*

James knew that people wouldn't think he was stupid when he asked for directions, but he still felt as though they thought badly of him when he needed to ask for assistance.

As he prepared to take his first step toward increasing his self-confidence, James brought to mind his ideal compassionate self and reminded himself of its qualities and attributes. He felt a sense of warmth and a gentle smile on his face. Inhabiting this image, he imagined himself standing on his local main street as people passed by. He imagined a middle-aged man thinking about his day ahead and rushing by, an older man reciting his shopping list to himself, a postwoman delivering letters, a family on the way to the bus, a teenager listening to music as she passed by. He imagined what was going on for them, what was running through their minds.

Then he imagined himself asking these people for directions to the nearest pharmacy. From his compassionate frame of mind, he reflected on what each person might think as they were interrupted in this way. He imagined that one person felt abruptly forced out of her daydreaming and put on the spot, being unable to think of where the pharmacy was; another felt slightly annoyed at having to stop for a moment; another did not seem to have any reaction; another felt positive about having a brief interaction with someone.

Doing this exercise helped James prepare for taking the first step toward his goal.

Exercise 46: Using Compassionate Imagery to Prepare for Any Situation

This exercise is similar to exercise 45 but can be used for both social and nonsocial situations.

Engage in your soothing-rhythm breathing or using your place-of-contentment imagery to promote a sense of soothing. When you are ready, bring to mind a compassionate image (coach, companion, or perfect nur-turer) or evoke the sense of your ideal compassionate self. Remind your-self of the key qualities of compassion. Feel a sense of warmth and allow a slight smile to appear on your face.

Now imagine the situation you are preparing for. Picture yourself in the situation. If you are imagining yourself as your ideal compassionate self, see the situation from this new perspective. Or imagine that your coach, companion, or perfect nurturer is supporting you in this situation. Feel a sense of strength and courage from this image.

Now, observe yourself having successfully completed the task. Imagine how this feels in your mind and body. This feeling may be one of strength or excitement; you may feel a broadening across your chest or a sense of warmth. Now observe yourself doing the task, feeling a sense of strength and courage. If you can imagine yourself suffering a setback, take time to experience the support provided by your ideal compassionate self or compassionate image.

Spend some time imagining the scene. Where appropriate, use your senses to make the scene come to life. What do you smell? What can you see? What sounds can you hear? What kind of helpful thoughts and images might occupy your mind in this situation?

Once you feel as though you have explored this imagery sufficiently, return to your soothing-rhythm breathing or your compassionate imagery and let the scene fade from your mind.

After a few minutes gently bring your awareness to the end of the exercise and become more aware of your physical environment.

• Hazel's Story

Hazel had self-confidence in a range of situations, but she found doing things on her own very difficult. She wasn't in a relationship and desperately wanted to go traveling, something she thought she would never be able to do on her own. When the company she worked for was taken over, she had the opportunity to go on to a trip to Canada. None of her friends was free to go along, so this meant that she had to decide whether to go on her own or not at all.

Some of Hazel's concerns centered around what people would think of her being on her own. She thought they would pity her, think she must be weird and have no friends. Other worries were concerned with being in "the great outdoors" on her own and being on her own in her hotel room at night.

She went ahead and booked her airline tickets and, in the weeks leading up to the trip, set herself some smaller steps to help her feel more self-confident. Among other things, she decided to go for a picnic on her own into the local countryside, go to the cinema to see an obscure film (at a time when she knew there wouldn't be people she knew around), and plan a night away at a hostel not too far from where she lived.

Before each of these activities, Hazel imagined herself into the situation in the company of her compassionate coach. She imagined her coach supporting and encouraging her, which helped her evoke a sense of strength and courage before taking each new step. When the step involved interacting with other people, she also used her compassionate mindset to imagine what might be in their minds at the time, a technique she found very helpful. After doing this for only a short time, Hazel was already starting to feel empowered. She noticed that in situations she had previously found daunting, she was better able to draw on her inner strength, even when she wasn't consciously trying. She also noticed that her posture had changed, and she actually found herself enjoying the new experiences she had set out to accomplish. The more she practiced, and the more steps she took, the more her self-confidence grew. The final tasks she had set for herself were actually easier to achieve than the first few, and though she still was occasionally anxious, the anticipation she experienced prior to new situations was almost a pleasurable feeling rather than a crippling one.

Reflection on Exercises 45 and 46

Because these exercises require you to imagine yourself in difficult situations, you may experience some uncomfortable feelings as you perform them. This is perfectly normal. When you notice difficult feelings, thoughts, and physical sensations, be mindful of them. If it helps, return to your soothing-rhythm breathing or compassionate imagery. Once you are more centered, resume the exercise.

Some people report initial feelings of skepticism about the usefulness of these exercises. However, time and time again, people report that once they are in the actual situation, having prepared for it in this way helps them to maintain a broader perspective. They feel supported and become less focused on feelings of threat or insecurity.

Exercise 47: Using Compassionate Alternative Thoughts and Images to Prepare for Taking Action

The compassionate-mind approach offers a range of strategies and techniques, which you can use separately or together, to build your self-confidence. If you find that obstacles to your progress arise in the form of negative thoughts or images, return to chapter 10 and use your compassionate alternative thoughts and images from worksheet 7 to help you resolve this.

Exercise 48: Using Compassionate Letter Writing to Access Inner Support

By now you may have developed your own way of approaching compassionate letter writing. This may involve sitting in a certain place at a specific time with a particular pen and notebook or journal. You may first use a mindfulness, breathing, or imagery exercise to evoke a compassionate frame of mind and use a particular scent, piece of music, or other such strategy. Whatever way you prepare to engage in this exercise, what is important is to use the prompts that are most helpful to you.

Now, from the perspective of the ideal compassionate self, your compassionate coach or companion, or perfect nurturer, put pen to paper and write a supportive letter to yourself in preparation for the action you are planning to take. It would help if the letter acknowledges the difficulty of your goal, wishes you the strength and courage to see it through, and reminds you that this is a new chapter in your life where you can experiment with situations and find out more about your inner strength and capabilities.

You may want to revisit the guiding principles for compassionate letter writing in chapter 11 to help you with this exercise.

• *Hazel's Story Continued*

Before Hazel went for a picnic on her own she wrote the following:

> *What you are planning to do tomorrow is going to be difficult, but you will get through it. Of course you are going to be anxious...breathe and observe the anxiety as it increases and decreases...try not to get caught up in it. If you get overly anxious, try to remember that it's not your fault...it may help to do an imagery exercise or soothing-rhythm breathing. This is one step further toward your holiday to Canada, which is likely to be one of the most empowering things you have done to date in your life. This is a step further toward a new, more self-confident you.*

As you have seen, compassionate letters can take all sorts of forms. Here Hazel wrote as if someone were cheering her on, being encouraging yet supportive, however the experiment turned out.

Exercise 49: Preparing for a Compassionate Behavioral Experiment

In final preparation for taking action, it often helps to think of what you're about to do as a compassionate behavioral experiment.

The following worksheet will help you clarify what you are about to do and remind you of why it may be helpful to take such an action. It will help you anticipate obstacles and ways of dealing with them. While some people find that they easily complete this worksheet in a self-supporting style, others find that spending a little time engaging in breathing or imagery exercises prior to tackling it helps them establish an appropriate compassionate mindset. Do whatever feels right.

Fill in the blanks after each statement. Take time to reflect on each part of this. James's worksheet, which follows, may serve as a guide.

Worksheet 11: Preparing for a Compassionate Behavioral Experiment

The step I am now going to take is: _____

_____

_____

_____

The things I can do to help me prepare for this are: _____

_____

_____

_____

The potential obstacles I can see are: _____

_____

_____

_____

I can do the following things to help me negotiate the obstacles: _____

_____

_____

_____

The things it would be helpful for me to remember just before and during the situation are: _____

_____

_____

_____

The additional things I can do to help me in the situation are: _____

_____

_____

_____

The things it would be helpful to tell myself after I have taken this step are:

_____

_____

_____

James's Worksheet: Preparing for a Compassionate Behavioral Experiment

The step I am now going to take is to go to the main street and ask for directions.

The things I can do to help me prepare for this are:

- Use compassionate imagery, both in relation to seeing people from a different perspective and in evoking a sense of strength from my compassionate coach.

- *Write a compassionate letter to myself to reflect on what I am about to do.*

- *Arrange to see one of my friends afterward so, no matter how it goes, I will have something to look forward to.*

- *Before going out, have a shower and make sure I have something I feel comfortable wearing, since both things generally make me feel better about myself.*

The potential obstacles I can see are:

- *I may start to panic and become lost for words.*

- *People may ignore me.*

- *I may chicken out.*

I can do the following things to help me negotiate the obstacles:

- *I can use my soothing-rhythm breathing if I get panicky.*

- *I can do some mindfulness or imagery exercises.*

- *If people ignore me, I can tell myself it may be nothing to do with me.*

- *I can tell myself that not everyone is going to be friendly and concentrate my efforts on finding someone helpful.*

- *If I feel the urge to avoid the situation, I can remind myself that this is just an experiment and a step further toward the things I want to achieve in life.*

The things it would be helpful for me to remember just before and during the situation are:

- *This is going to help me learn about myself; whichever way it goes, it will help me develop my self-confidence because I will know more at the end of it.*

- *Afterward, I can give myself a pat on the back for facing the things I am fearful of.*

- *I can always revert to my soothing-rhythm breathing, take a break, or use some imagery if it is difficult.*

- *Other people struggle as I do. It's not just me.*

- *There are many things that I can do. It is good to bring them to mind.*

The additional things I can do to help myself in the situation are:

- *I can assume a relaxed and open, yet confident, posture.*

- *Keep a smooth pebble in my pocket to help me if a difficult situation arises, for I've found that manipulating a smooth pebble has helped me in some of the imagery exercises.*

The things it would be helpful to tell myself after I have taken this step are:

- *Whatever the outcome, facing this is an achievement. It shows I have courage.*

- *It is okay to renegotiate the steps and rethink things if they don't go according to plan.*

- *If things don't go according to plan, I will at least know more and can then go through this process again.*

- *This is worth the effort I am putting in, no matter what the outcome is.*

- *Building something is hard and takes time.*

- *I can be proud of myself for attempting to do this.*

Reflection on Exercises 48 and 49

Some people find that these preparatory exercises are best done in the order set out in this chapter, while others prefer doing things in a different sequence. Choose whatever works best for you.

It's good to try all of these exercises, but if want to design your own to do instead, that's okay too. It may be that you find that you need little preparation in the early stages but more as you work up to more difficult tests of your self-confidence. Alternatively, some people find that the early exercises help prepare them for the later ones.

DOING AND REVIEWING

Finally you have reached the part of the book that involves "doing" or experimenting with situations. It is hoped that you already will have experienced changes in your level of self-confidence, but this stage marks a significant advance.

Exercise 50: Doing Your Compassionate Behavioral Experiment

Compassionate behavioral experiments are exactly that: experiments. So now it's time to take the steps you've been preparing for. If possible, view taking these steps as a means to find out more about yourself or other people. Remember, information is power. Ironically, the steps you take here are likely to be incredibly big ones, and yet this is the shortest section of the chapter—if not the book!

Exercise 51: Reviewing Your Compassionate Behavioral Experiment

Use the following worksheet to review the action you have taken in your compassionate behavioral experiment. It may be helpful at first to complete this worksheet in a spontaneous way and then to revisit it after practicing an exercise that evokes a compassionate frame of mind. Your resulting perspective may enable you to add more to the worksheet. Fill in the blanks to complete each of the following statements.

Worksheet 12: Reflections on Your Compassionate Behavioral Experiment

The step I took was: _____

_____

_____

_____

How it went in general: _____

_____

_____

_____

The things I learned about myself through this exercise were: _____

_____

_____

_____

The things I learned about other people through this exercise were: ____

_____

_____

_____

The things it would be helpful for me to remember just before and during such situations are: _____

_____

_____

_____

The potential adjustments that I could make in such situations in the future are: _____

_____

_____

_____

In summary: _____

_____

_____

_____

Taking all of this into account, it may be helpful for me to do the following to build my self-confidence further: _____

_____

_____

_____

After her compassionate behavioral experiment, Hazel reviewed her experience and completed this worksheet.

Hazel's Worksheet: Reflections on Her Compassionate Behavioral Experiment

The step I took was to stay a night in a hostel on my own.

How it went in general: Things went well. I was really anxious at first, but I got to my room and settled in. I met some people in the communal area who seemed nice. Some were with other people; some were on their own. There just seemed to be an acceptance from everyone, regarding what other people were doing/why they were there.

There was one girl who seemed a bit aloof, but I then engaged with some imagery exercises and that helped me think about what might be going on for her. She might have been anxious or maybe not interested in talking, and that is okay.

Breakfast was a bit awkward, as I ended up sitting by myself because there was no room at the larger table, but I read my book and practiced some mindfulness exercises.

The things I learned about myself through this exercise were:

- Although it was anxiety provoking at times, I proved that I could do it. I have more courage than I thought.

- I can enjoy time on my own—it was quite liberating.

The things I learned about other people through this exercise were:

- Other people stay on their own at hostels.

- People did not seem to judge me in any way.

- A group of girls ended up chatting to me in the kitchen and said they had met up while traveling alone.

- *People are nicer than I thought; in fact, there were other people like me.*

- *There are always going to be people around that I don't get along with; that's normal.*

The things it would be helpful for me to remember just before and during such situations are:

- *All of the above, but also that it is worthwhile experimenting with situations. Experimenting is actually quite exciting.*

- *Things hardly ever go perfectly, but they can still be worthwhile.*

- *At this moment in time, I feel a lot more confident. This will fade, but I need to savor it and remind myself of this just before I put myself in another situation.*

The potential adjustments that I could make in such situations in the future are:

- *When I stay in a hostel again, it may be good to go into the communal areas more often, maybe sitting and reading, maybe chatting.*

- *I don't need to explain myself. If people ask, I could maybe just say, "Yes, I am traveling alone; none of my friends could get the time off."*

- *It's okay to stay in my room as well if I feel like it. It doesn't make me sad. It just makes me human.*

In summary: This exercise was so liberating. I am so glad I did it. The experiment allowed me to visit a different place and have a great experience. Yes, it was difficult at times, but that is okay. It is the first time I have done it, and I can learn from it, making the next visit better. I can cope with anxiety-provoking situations, and they don't have to stop me from living my life.

Taking all of this into account, it may be helpful for me to do the following to build my self-confidence further:

- *Stay at another hostel for a weekend, somewhere less familiar.*

- *Afterward, tell people that I have been away for a weekend by myself, staying in a hostel, and see what they say. Evoke strength and courage from my compassionate coach before I tell them so I can feel empowered, as opposed to awkward and apologetic. After all, it was fun, and even if I have offers of company, I may still decide to do it on my own at times.*

Reflection on Exercise 51

It may be helpful to use worksheet 12 exactly as it is or you may wish to customize it. Either way is fine. In addition, you may find it helpful to use this material as the basis for a compassionate letter. Try it and see if it helps.

CONCLUSIONS

In this chapter, you have looked at taking action by means of compassionate behavior. In fact, all the things you have done so far in this book could be classified this way, but the exercises outlined in this chapter will hopefully have helped you make additional self-compassionate behavioral changes that will help build your self-confidence.

Chapter 13 will look at some other ways to help you take action, such as using assertiveness techniques and making small (or big) changes that may further benefit you in your everyday life.

13

Additional Strategies to Help Build Your Self-Confidence

Courage does not always roar. Sometimes courage is the quiet voice at
the end of the day saying, "I will try again tomorrow."

—Mary Anne Radmacher

In this penultimate chapter you will learn a number of additional ways
to help build your self-confidence. The chapter will cover:

- Assertiveness strategies

- Making seemingly small behavioral changes

- Savoring positive experiences

- Acceptance

- Using self-compassion to guide your day

- Using self-compassion to help you in difficult situations

You can use some of the following exercises in combination with others you have already tried, or you can use these exercises on their own. The important thing is to find what is effective for you.

Each of the exercises covered in this chapter can be found on your personal practice summary sheet, which you can continue to use as a space for reflection and summary.

ASSERTIVENESS STRATEGIES

Being assertive means being able to express ourselves while also being respectful of the views, feelings, and needs of others. This may include expressing our emotions, needs, and points of view. When we assertively express ourselves, we are being neither apologetic nor aggressive. Assertiveness is about finding a state in between. While some people who struggle with assertiveness fluctuate between two extremes (for example, acting first aggressive then submissive), others find that they almost always follow the same pattern, tending to one or the other every time.

Sometimes people think that to be assertive they must know how they are feeling, have a clear point of view, or be able to identify a specific need. However, at times assertiveness means expressing a mixture of emotions. It can involve saying "I don't know," "I don't care," or "I don't know what I need." Equally, assertiveness may be deciding not to show our emotions or share our views, thoughts, and needs, if we don't want to do so. Confusing, isn't it? Basically, assertiveness is about our acknowledging how we think, how we feel, what we need, and what we want to do and, in the process, respecting ourselves and others.

Assertiveness can be a consequence of or can help build self-confidence. It is a learned skill and one that we can develop. Hopefully, some of the exercises covered so far will have helped you build your own capacity to be assertive. These exercises may have helped you gain a better understanding of yourself and others, and understanding our situation and that of other people can help us feel less ashamed and more empowered.

It is hoped that the mindfulness exercises, soothing-rhythm breathing, and, in particular, the imagery exercises have already given you a sense of strength and courage. In addition, working on compassionate alternative thoughts and images, letter writing, and especially compassionate behavioral experiments is also likely to have improved your ability to assert yourself. This chapter will give you some assertiveness strategies that will enhance what you've already learned.

• *Sarah's Story*

Sarah used to feel that she was not taken seriously at work. Her boss seemed to ignore her needs as an employee. She did not have a regular computer to use and found that this impacted her job, half of which involved data input. Constantly hovering near the desks of her coworkers, looking for a computer to borrow, had a negative effect on her relationships at work.

For months she tried to broach the subject with her boss. She tried to do this subtly and indirectly. On the way to the coffee room, she tentatively mentioned to him, "There's most likely nothing you can do, but it would be nice for me to have a computer that I could use regularly. I do know that space is cramped and other people have priority." Sarah desperately wanted her boss to pick up on what she was trying to say, but instead he simply responded, "Yeah, it's a bit cramped, the building's not good," as he left the room.

Similar conversations occurred for several months. When she mentioned to her partner what was going on at work, he became angry and responded, "You should just go in and tell him it's not good enough." Sarah had mixed feelings about this. On the one hand, her partner had validated that it was unacceptable for her not to have her own computer, and she felt fired up enough to go in and say something, but on the other hand, it made her feel like a wimp that she had done nothing before this. Eventually, she took up the issue with her boss again.

With a tremor in her voice she asked, "May I have a word with you?" After receiving no response, she raised her voice slightly: "John, I need to speak to you." Her boss turned around. She said, "I need a computer I can use whenever I choose. You obviously don't take me seriously enough to give me one, and that make me feel like rubbish. Everyone I have spoken to thinks it's outrageous that I haven't gotten one."

As you can imagine, her words were met with a defensive response from John. He asked, *"What side of the bed did you wake up on?"* thus locating the problem firmly in her court. A heated discussion followed, resulting in Sarah being lectured about her bad attitude.

If only Sarah had known the assertiveness strategies she later learned to use. It was too late for that job, but the strategies she subsequently learned held her in good stead in other workplaces.

Expressing Your Feelings, Needs, and Points of View

Sometimes the way we let people know our views or how we feel seems to increase the likelihood of a negative outcome, such as provoking an argument or not being taken seriously. We may be too passive or too aggressive in our approach to others, which has the same disappointing effect. It is therefore helpful to work out ways in which we can express our feelings, needs, and points of view in an assertive manner.

An *I-message* can prove very helpful to this end. You could start with this construction:

I think/feel/need _____ . *This is based on* _____

_____ .

I think it would be helpful if _____ .
Can we discuss this?

Alternatively, you could construct what you have to say as follows:

When you do/say _____ , *I feel* _____

_____

and I would prefer _____ .
Can we discuss this?

As you can see, the first of these two constructions addresses your own needs, feelings, or thoughts first, while the second construction turns this around and puts the other person's actions or words first and expresses your feelings afterward. Indeed, there is no right and wrong way to approach assertiveness. What is important is to find something that works for you and seems to go with how you might say something naturally.

Finishing with the question "Can we discuss this?" acknowledges that the other person may have important thoughts and feelings too.

The following are examples of how an I-message might work in practice:

1. "*I think* I am not being taken seriously at work *because* none of the ideas I come up with in meetings are ever acted upon. *I think it would be helpful if* you could give me feedback after meetings about any ideas I have expressed so that I can understand why they may not be viable. *Can we discuss this?*"

2. "When you leave the house in a mess, *I feel* as though you don't care about me and just expect me to clean up after you. *I would prefer it* if you tidied up after yourself or tell me why this is difficult for you so I can understand it better. *Can we discuss this?*"

3. "*I need* to have some time to myself every so often. *This is because* I get stressed when life is so busy. *I would like* a little bit of free time, as it would make me happier and more relaxed, and would make me feel cared for by you. I am not sure what you think. *Can we discuss this?*"

As you can see from these examples, there are many ways you can use this assertiveness strategy. It also is okay for you to vary the wording. For example, it may be that you replace "based on" with "because," or "I would prefer" with "I would like," as different terms may seem more natural to you.

When you say "I feel," it leaves less opportunity for people to disagree with you. This is in stark contrast to such statements as "You make me..." or "You are making me feel...," which are more likely to trigger disagreement. That is, using I-messages, in contrast to *you-messages*, is more likely to lead to agreement.

These new ways of expressing yourself may seem difficult to remember, especially in situations where you feel strong emotions, such as anger or anxiety, but the more you practice them, the more naturally they will come to mind. Practicing may involve writing down what you want to say or saying it out loud when you are on your own. It may involve practicing in front of other people who have your best interests at heart and can give you constructive feedback. Some people find practicing in front of a mirror very helpful. Most of all, trying it out, maybe initially in easier situations and building up to more difficult ones, can help you hone this way of expressing yourself so that eventually it begins to roll off your tongue quite naturally.

Once you have practiced what you want to say, a further component of the exercise, one with which you will be very familiar by now, is to evoke a supportive frame of mind to help you say what you want to say. Self-assertiveness may be anxiety provoking, at least until it becomes a regular part of your life. So, before you approach the person with whom you wish to assert yourself, engage in your soothing-rhythm breathing for a minute or so. When you are ready, bring to mind a compassionate image or evoke the sense of your ideal compassionate self. Remind yourself of the key compassionate qualities. Feel a sense of warmth and calm, together with strength and courage. Adjust your posture, feeling strength in your spine and openness and warmth in your facial expression. Now approach the person and say what you have been planning and practicing to say.

Using a Hook to Motivate Others to Change Their Behavior

Unfortunately, despite your best efforts, other people may not change their behavior. This may be because they can't do it or because they find it too difficult. However, it may be because they are not able to empathize with your situation or because they need to see what's in it for them. If you find yourself in this situation, it may be helpful to add a so-called hook to the exercise. In other words, tell them what's in it for them. For example, a change in their behavior may mean you will be less anxious, and therefore you would be easier to be around; it may build your self-confidence so you can take on more roles at work; it may mean that you feel more valued and therefore seek reassurance from them less.

Exercise 52: Communicating How You Feel and What Your Needs Are

Take the following steps to communicate assertively:

Step 1: Bring to mind a situation where you were having difficulty expressing yourself.

Step 2: Using an I-message, work out what you want to say and how you can say it.

Step 3: Plan when you are going to speak to the person.

Step 4: Practice, whether on your own, with someone you trust, or in front of the mirror.

Step 5: Make use of exercises you have found helpful in the past. For example, prepare for this as a compassionate behavioral experiment, write a compassionate letter to yourself, or sit in the presence of your compassionate coach to gain strength and encouragement.

Step 6: Express yourself to the person in question.

Step 7: Review how this exercise went using worksheet 12, writing a compassionate letter to yourself, or using compassionate imagery, especially if things did not go quite as you had hoped.

Reflection on Exercise 52

There will be situations that you cannot plan for or be proactive about. You may be put on the spot and need to react or say something quickly. In such situations, it is helpful to take a soothing breath, then feel strength in your spine and, if you can, express yourself in an assertive manner. The more you do this, the more naturally these steps will come to you.

Unfortunately, many of us find that others often resist the changes we are trying to make. People get used to our being a particular way and interact with us accordingly. This can be very frustrating. If you find this is the case for you, it may be worth addressing the issue as Linda did.

- *Linda's Story*

When Linda tried being more assertive at work, things generally
went the way she had hoped. However, when she tried it with her
partner, he simply responded, "Have you been reading some of
that self-help again?" In addition, one of her sisters just shrugged
her shoulders and said she did not have the time to discuss things.
Linda therefore thought long and hard about this and finally
responded to her partner: "When you say things like that to me, it
hurts because I feel as though you don't want me to be more self-
confident. I am trying my best. It would be great if you could help
me with this because I think it would be good for me and for our
relationship. Can we discuss this?"

  With her sister, she felt as though she could not take another
direct snub again, so instead she emailed her: "I know you said
you did not have time to discuss things with me, but this only
makes me feel more sure that you don't value me as a friend and
sister. It would be good if you could spare some time to talk, but
if you can't, that is okay, as well. At least I can say that I have
tried." Both strategies resulted in positive outcomes. With her
partner, the conversation brought them closer together. He started
to take an interest in the changes that Linda was trying to make
and, in addition, changed his own behavior toward her. He even
started to use this way of expressing himself at home and at work.

  With Linda's sister, nothing changed. She did not even
respond to the email, but Linda felt proud that she had stood
her ground in this way. She reassured herself every so often by
thinking, "This is about her, not me. I have tried, but I'm not
going to bang my head against a brick wall."

Exercise 53: Giving Constructive Feedback

Most of us fear upsetting other people, and this can prevent us from giving
constructive feedback, which may result in our avoiding an issue entirely or
skirting around it. It can also lead to frustration with other people (and with
ourselves) as patterns of behavior go on repeating themselves.

Although the previous exercise may be helpful in such situations, other relationships require us to be less focused on our own needs, feelings, and views and more receptive to the needs of someone else or, in work situations, an organization or company.

If you find giving constructive feedback difficult, work through the steps below.

Step 1: Think about the person to whom you wish to give some constructive feedback and bring to mind the specific issue in question.

Step 2: Take a few breaths and bring to mind a compassionate image or your ideal compassionate self; remind yourself of the key compassionate qualities: strength and courage but, importantly here, empathy and nonjudgment also.

Step 3: Remind yourself that you wish the other person to be the best that he or she can be. You wish to help this person's development.

Step 4: Now think what this person needs to know, employing the following I-message: "I want you to know that…It is important that I tell you this because…Can we discuss this?"

Step 5: Now plan how and when you are going to give your feedback.

Step 6: Practice on your own, with someone you trust, or in front of the mirror.

Step 7: Make use of exercises you have found helpful in the past. For example, use worksheet 11 to help prepare you for implementing your plan. This is likely to include what you are going to do in the moments before you speak to the person in question, writing a compassionate letter to yourself, or sitting in the presence of your compassionate coach to gain strength and encouragement.

Step 8: Express yourself to the person in question.

Step 9: Review how it went using worksheet 12. Write a compassionate letter to yourself with respect to this exercise or use compassionate imagery, especially if things did not go quite as you had hoped.

•   *Isaac's Story*

Isaac found that one of the new members of his team, Andrew, regularly arrived late for work. At first Isaac ignored it, thinking his coworker must have had problems predicting the traffic, and told himself that eventually things would sort themselves out. But as time went on, the problem continued. Isaac started hovering around reception at the time that Andrew usually arrived and looking at the clock as he approached the office, but this did not seem to have any effect at all. Isaac became increasingly angry with Andrew while also being annoyed with himself, thinking Stand up for yourself. You're pathetic. *Isaac found that when he had to interact with Andrew, he was short with him, and he tended to look at Andrew's work with a more critical eye than was warranted. It got to the point where he could not be around the other man in the cafeteria or coffee room.*

This was clearly not a good situation for Isaac, Andrew, or for others on his team. They could see someone getting away with coming in late, felt resentful themselves, and were aware of tension in the work environment.

In this situation Isaac could have used the strategy outlined in exercise 52 above, but it seemed inappropriate to be talking about his own needs, feelings, and thoughts in this situation. Instead, he decided it would be beneficial to give Andrew some constructive feedback. That evening he used imagery to remind himself of the key compassionate qualities, especially courage, empathy, and nonjudgment, and he thought about Andrew from this perspective. I want him to be the best that he can be, *Isaac thought.*

He imagined himself saying to Andrew, "I want you to know that the working day starts at 9:00 a.m., and yet I have noticed that you regularly arrive later than that. It is important that we discuss this because it has an impact on the work you do, the rest of the team, and also on you, as well. Can we discuss it?"

Once Isaac had imagined himself saying this, he realized that it might be best to have the discussion away from the main part of the office and potential interruptions, allowing space and time for it. He ran through what he was going to say a few times and used compassionate imagery and soothing-rhythm breathing to recruit the appropriate frame of mind, one that would be nonjudgmental, warm, empathic, and strong. The night before he planned to have the discussion, Isaac used worksheet 11 to help him think through what he was about to do and also wrote a letter to himself in his journal.

The next day Isaac carefully followed his plan. He engaged in his breathing exercise, reminded himself of the key compassionate qualities, and, with warmth in his face and voice, asked to speak to Andrew. After he had said what he had to say, he calmly waited for a response. Andrew paused. It seemed that the air of calm that Isaac had adopted had rubbed off on him and he sat quietly for a few moments. He then responded, "Yes, I know I am terrible at keeping track of time and am usually late. All I can say is I am sorry and I will make a concerted effort from here on in." After a discussion of the practicalities of his getting in on time, Andrew got up to leave and on the way out stated, "Thanks for being so good about it. I will do better."

Reflection on Exercise 53

Giving constructive feedback may involve your working through some of the strategies you have tried before, such as coming up with compassionate alternative thoughts and images, writing a compassionate letter to yourself, and preparing for a compassionate behavioral experiment. By now, you will know what other exercises may be helpful to you to supplement this exercise.

Remember that if you are giving constructive feedback from a compassionate mindset, you are doing it with the other person's best interests at heart. This is being like a compassionate teacher, whose role is to nurture others to be the best they can be, which involves giving feedback without judgment. Turning the focus from ourselves to what other people need so they can grow and be their best can give us the strength and courage to act. It obviously has a huge impact on our own self-confidence also.

MAKING SEEMINGLY SMALL BEHAVIORAL CHANGES

This book has focused on increasing your self-confidence, and now that you are hopefully building your self-confidence, you may find that making small behavioral changes can have a positive effect on your own happiness and that of others. Doing this can further develop your self-confidence, directly or indirectly.

Here are a few ideas that people have previously found beneficial:

- Sign up to help a campaign or volunteer for something you believe in.

- Make some changes to your home environment. This may involve buying a plant or some flowers, putting a photo up that reminds you of good times or important relationships, tidying up the house or your garden.

- Engage in brief opportunities for mindfulness, such as mindful hand washing, stretching, or drinking.

- At certain points in the day or when triggered by certain events, encourage yourself to stop, drop your shoulders, and take a soothing breath.

- Go for a walk and say hello to someone as you walk down the street. If you can manage only a fleeting smile at first, try gradually to increase this to holding the other person's gaze for slightly longer next time.

- When you pay the cashier at the store, make sure you make some eye contact and small talk.

- Watch a film that makes you laugh or gives you a sense of warmth.

- Experiment with new situations just to see what happens.

- Make an effort to help someone in your neighborhood who is in need of it.

- Give some things that you no longer need to charity and savor the act of giving.

- Engage in a random act of kindness, maybe to someone you know, maybe to a stranger; this can range from a kind word to a warm gesture.

- Do something that you used to enjoy doing. This does not have to be something you have enjoyed as an adult. It may be something you enjoyed as a child, such as going to the fair, sitting on the beach, drawing, sewing, or riding your bike.

- Have a look around and see whether you can draw inspiration from other people. How are they spending their time?

If you decide to make behavioral changes, it may be beneficial to use the following guidelines.

Mix It Up

Engage in a range of new behaviors over time rather than picking only one or two and sticking to them. Research tells us that we habituate, or quickly get used to, the positive benefits of any activity. For example, you may really appreciate a new plant you have bought for a room, but after a week or two, it is likely that you'll come to take it for granted and gain less pleasure from seeing it. Similarly, you may get a buzz from having a positive encounter with someone for the first time, but ten encounters later it may feel less rewarding.

Incorporate Changes into Your Daily Life, But Don't Let Them Become a Chore

One study split a number of students into two groups. Group A was instructed to do five random acts of kindness all in one day, while group B was told to do one random act of kindness per day over five days. At the end of the experiment, group A was found to be significantly happier than group B. One interpretation of these findings is that instructing participants to do one act per day increased the likelihood that the practice became a chore. Therefore, if you find that what you've planned to do is becoming a chore, stop doing it. Instead, it may be helpful to take stock and adjust your plans.

Although the study was looking at happiness per se, I would suggest that those whose level of happiness is increased are likely to feel more self-confident as a result.

• *Andy's Story Continued*

Andy had slowly and methodically worked through all the stages of the compassionate-mind approach to building his self-confidence and had developed a tool kit of practices and strategies that he found helpful. He was surprised that he had found the strength to tackle a number of difficult things both at work and in his personal life and felt as though his main focus should be on practicing certain mindfulness and imagery exercises (self-practice) to maintain and strengthen the gains he had made. Andy recognized that much of this work was directed at developing self-compassion further to regulate his still sensitive threat system.

Andy did, however, feel an urge to see how else he could consciously change his life in the pursuit of more pleasure. He reflected that he had avoided so many things in the past because of his lack of self-confidence. He felt that he'd been driven to prove himself and to keep his mind away from thinking about his past, but now he was motivated toward experimenting in potentially positive ways. Andy started to write reminders in his journal to do certain things. These included "random act of kindness day," "karaoke night," "new situation day," "funny film night," and "hello-to-five-people-in-the-street day." He reflected that he would find some of these things relatively easy, while others filled him with dread.

Some days he achieved his goals without much preparation, while others took a considerable amount of time and energy. Two weeks later, Andy reflected that he felt more positive. He felt a sense of achievement and, because he had continued his self-practice, felt content within himself and around other people. Some of the exercises he'd been doing had a direct effect on his self-confidence, while others seemed to be working indirectly.

Exercise 54: Making
Seemingly Small Changes

Do the following:

Step 1: Put together a list of things you think it would be good to do.

Step 2: Allocate tasks to specific days of the week.

Step 3: Prepare for the activities using exercises you've found helpful in the past.

Step 4: Engage in the activities.

Step 5: If it is helpful, review the resulting experiences in your notebook or journal or use worksheet 12.

Reflection on Exercise 54

Making small behavioral changes can be a positive and uplifting experience, but take care to maintain and further develop your contentment and soothing system at the same time. Remember, our drive and resource acquisition system is powerful and can give us a real buzz and sense of achievement. But you need to keep all three of your emotional systems in balance. Working on one to the detriment or neglect of another can lead to coming unstuck when things maybe don't go quite according to plan. Self-compassion will support you through the difficult times, as well as help you build resilience for life's inevitable setbacks.

SAVORING POSITIVE EXPERIENCES

Life can be so busy that it is all too easy to spend the majority of our time thinking about what we have got to do next or what we have just done. Consciously savoring our positive experiences in the moment can enhance their emotional impact. It can also help create a more vivid memory store on which we can draw at a later date, turning a conscious moment of contentment or happiness into many more such moments.

Savoring positive experiences is a very simple strategy that involves stopping and appreciating a particular point in time. You could savor the sense of achievement you get when you have successfully faced a difficult situation. You could savor a moment of exhilaration, a moment of clarity, a moment of awe as you look upon some beautiful scenery, or a moment when you feel really connected to those around you. You may also choose to savor the experience of being in freshly changed bed linen or the experience of sipping a welcome hot drink, stepping inside a warm house and closing the door on a wintry evening, or stretching after arising from a restful night's sleep.

Because the exercises you are completing throughout this book are aimed at building your self-confidence, it may perhaps be a good thing to concentrate on savoring these experiences in particular. For instance, you may want to savor the sense of achievement you get after you have engaged in a compassionate behavioral experiment or the positive feedback you receive when something has gone well. But, of course, it equally may be helpful to you to savor a whole range of situations, big and small. Choose whatever works best for you.

Exercise 55: Savoring Positive Experiences

Step 1: Notice a positive experience or stop to appreciate a moment in time, no matter how small.

Step 2: Take a soothing breath and relax your shoulders.

Step 3: Appreciate the moment.

Step 4: Work through your senses. What can you see, hear, smell, feel, and taste? Linger on each of these sensations in turn.

Step 5: When you are ready, take another soothing breath and return your attention to your surroundings.

Reflection on Exercise 55

Savoring is similar to mindfulness in that it encourages you to be in the moment. However, while mindfulness focuses more on observing, or at least this was the way it was used in chapter 7, savoring involves appreciating moments in time and experiencing a sense of warmth while doing so.

Many people find that they can strengthen the positive effects of savoring by regularly recording in their journals particular moments that they have savored. Later recalling such positive experiences, especially when we are feeling low or anxious, can help lift our mood. Some people find that taking a photograph of something they are savoring will act to boost their mood, both at the time and in the future. This is why so many of us tend to have photos around to capture and remind us of particular experiences. But remember, it would be a good idea to savor a whole range of experiences and to change your display of photos from time to time, as they can lose their evocative power.

ACCEPTANCE

In life, there are things that we can change and adjust and things that, no matter how hard we try, we are unable to do anything about. It is likely that you have become more aware of this while working your way through this book. For example, you may have surprised yourself by now being able to do certain things that you previously felt were impossible for you. However, this may be accompanied by a feeling of sadness that you were unable to do such things in the past. In addition you may be aware that things such as your fundamental appearance or certain aspects of your personality are also difficult, if not impossible, to change.

The concept and, more importantly, the feeling of acceptance can help us come to terms with such things. Acceptance is not about being defeated. Instead, it can be a very powerful state of mind, a strong foundation upon which to base new developments in our lives.

Although it is useful to develop acceptance of the things we cannot change, it can also be helpful to develop acceptance of how things are for you at present.

The "Perfect" Illusion

One of the reasons people suffer with poor self-confidence is because they try—and fail—to be perfect. When they don't achieve what they set out to do, they give themselves a hard time. If you think this may be the case for you, ask yourself the question: *Would I like someone who was perfect?*

I personally find it difficult to be around people whom I perceive as perfect. I can easily be intimidated by them, and as a consequence, I don't tend to feel good about myself while I'm around them.

If I think back to times in my life when an acquaintance has become a friend, it has usually come about when something has happened to show that this person is a human being who is not perfect. For example, when "perfect" Amy let me know that she was struggling with work and was worried about it, things between us changed. She turned from being someone with whom I engaged in social chitchat to someone I had a connection with. Her admission made me see her as a human being. I felt flattered that she had confided in me. It gave me an opportunity to feel I was of help to her, and our friendship developed from that point.

To drive this message home further, in the film *Good Will Hunting*, Robin Williams's character defends his late wife by passionately stating that it was her idiosyncrasies and imperfections that made her perfect in his eyes. Watch the film if you haven't seen it. The message is delivered very powerfully. This is something I bring to mind whenever I find that self-criticism has been triggered in me. It helps me be self-compassionate and ultimately to accept myself, idiosyncrasies (and, boy, there are a lot of them!) and all.

Close consideration of things we cannot change can be emotionally draining. It may be helpful for you to work initially on things that are likely to produce relatively less powerful emotions. As you become more practiced in this way of working, you can move on to the things that are more challenging for you.

Exercise 56: Accepting Yourself and Things That You Cannot Change

As you have done with many of the previous exercises, find a place where you can be relatively undisturbed for ten to fifteen minutes or so, where you will be free from distractions, and where you feel comfortable to engage in an imagery exercise. Sit with strength in your spine, and with feelings of openness and warmth; bring a slight smile to your face.

Step 1: Bring to mind something that you wish you could change but cannot. You may choose something that happened in the past or something in the present.

Step 2: Engage with your soothing-rhythm breathing, and when you are ready, bring to mind your ideal compassionate self or a compassionate image. This may be your perfect nurturer, compassionate coach, or compassionate companion.

Step 3: Remind yourself of the key qualities of compassion, experiencing each of them in turn.

Step 4: Now bring your attention to the aspect of your life that you cannot change. Invite your ideal compassionate self or your compassionate coach, companion, or other role to recognize the disappointment you feel that change is not possible.

Step 5: Now think about what your ideal compassionate self or compassionate role might say about this. How would its voice sound? What emotions would it direct toward you? Are there colors, smells, or sounds associated with this experience? Consider this for a few minutes.

Step 6: If possible, experience a sensation of peace...a sense of calm, a sense of acceptance...once again allowing this to last for a while.

Step 7: When you are ready, return to your soothing-rhythm breathing and let the image and the experience fade from your mind, slowly bringing your awareness back to your surroundings.

Marie's story is an example of how this exercise helped someone accept problems with her appearance and achieve more self-confidence as a result.

• *Marie's Story*

Marie had lost her mother to cancer when she was only three years old and had later suffered at the hands of her stepmother. She was bullied at school and had had a couple of difficult relationships. It seemed as though her life after three years of age could be represented by the domino effect. The diagrammatic formulation and imagery exercises had helped her grieve and feel less anger about a number of things, but she felt she still had work to do.

Marie also identified that there were things in her present life that she wanted to change but couldn't. She was self-conscious about her appearance, more specifically her crooked smile and large nose. When she managed to ask people she cared about for feedback on this, they reacted kindly but confirmed that she did indeed have a crooked smile and a large nose. Despite this, she felt okay in their company, knowing they would love her whatever, but with other people, she felt extremely self-conscious and would bow her head, avoid smiling, and sometimes avoid social situations altogether.

Marie had found compassionate behavioral experiments very useful but still felt that she was struggling to accept her looks. She decided to work further on acceptance of her appearance. She brought to mind how she looked and imagined sitting in the presence of her compassionate coach. She imagined her compassionate coach gently cupping her face with two hands. She heard her coach softly say: "You are who you are...you are okay... there is no need to hang your head...feel the strength to hold your head up high...when things are difficult, take a breath...feel the warmth, the strength, and courage...face the world."

This exercise changed Marie's life dramatically. Although it brought her to tears at the time, she felt the strength and courage she needed to face the world in a spirit of self-acceptance. The other experiments she engaged in suddenly seemed easier to do, setbacks were easier to recover from, and her self-confidence grew.

Reflection on Exercise 56

As in the case of previous exercises, especially those using imagery, you may find that your self-critic attempts to undermine your efforts. If this is the case, remind your self-critic that you are both on the same team and that there are alternative and more helpful ways than self-criticism to achieve your goals.

This exercise may be difficult to undertake. You may want to plan to do something afterward for yourself as a reward. Have a warm bath, go for a walk, see a friend, put some uplifting music on, or take a nap.

Exercise 57: Embracing Who You Are

In contrast to the previous exercise, which is often associated with a sense of gentleness and warmth, people often find that embracing who they are is energizing. Of course, both exercises aim to help you feel a sense of inner strength.

Once again, start with something that is relatively easy for you and move on to things that are more difficult later.

Find a place where you can be undistracted for ten to fifteen minutes or so, one that is free from distractions and where you can comfortably engage in an imagery exercise.

Step 1: Bring to mind something that is associated with difficult feelings for you, something that you cannot change and have difficulty accepting. It may be an aspect of your appearance, part of your personality, something that has happened to you, or something that is going on at the moment.

Step 2: Now stand up. Feel strength and alertness in your spine. Engage in your soothing-rhythm breathing. With each breath, feel your chest expand. Adjust your posture to evoke strength.

Step 3: If it helps, inhabit your ideal compassionate self. Alternatively imagine your compassionate coach or companion or your perfect nurturer standing with you, maybe behind you, maybe alongside, with a hand on your shoulder.

Step 4: Now, with both warmth and strength, make a statement such as the following: "I am a human being who has amazing capacities and abilities. It is normal for me to struggle in certain areas and at certain times. I am human...I am not perfect...I have/am/have experienced _____ . It is understandable for me to have difficulty with this...But I am resilient and I can accept this about myself." Stay with this feeling for a while.

Step 5: When you are ready, return to your soothing-rhythm breathing. Once more, feel a sense of strength and alertness in your posture and your mind. Now let the experience fade, slowly bringing your awareness back to where you are standing.

Reflection on Exercise 57

During many of these exercises, it is beneficial to experience a balance of all of the key qualities of compassion. However, in this exercise it can be more helpful to focus on specific components of compassion, primarily strength and courage.

Here are a few statements that people have previously found helpful to use during this exercise:

"At this moment in time, I am not as self-confident as I would like to be."

"I am a survivor."

"I have survived difficult things."

"I am a shy person."

"I have a stammer."

"I have a big nose. So what?"

During the exercise, the aim is not to feel apologetic but rather to feel strength and a sense of self-confidence, even with respect to something that you usually find difficult to accept. Compassionate imagery may help you with this.

Adjusting your posture during the exercise, until you feel a sense of strength and self-confidence, can also be extremely helpful.

Exercise 58: Accepting Your Situation, Right Here, Right Now

This exercise is similar to the previous ones, but instead of focusing on something that you cannot or are unlikely to be able to change, the focus is on accepting where you find yourself right now.

Find a place where you can be relatively undisturbed for ten to fifteen minutes or so, a place that is free from distractions, where you feel comfortable to engage in an imagery exercise.

Step 1: While standing up, feel strength in your spine and a sense of alertness. Engage in your soothing-rhythm breathing. With each breath, feel your chest expand, and if it helps, adjust your posture to evoke a sense of strength.

Step 2: If it helps, imagine your ideal compassionate self or other compassionate role standing with you, maybe behind you, maybe alongside, with a hand on your shoulder.

Step 3: Now, with both warmth and strength, make a statement such as the following: "I am a human being who has amazing capacities and abilities...It is normal for me to struggle in certain areas and at certain times. I am human...I am not perfect, but I can accept myself for who I am right in this moment." Stay with this experience for a few moments.

Step 4: When you are ready, return to your soothing-rhythm breathing. Once more, feel a sense of strength and alertness in your posture and your mind. Now let the experience fade, slowly bringing your awareness back to where you are standing.

Reflection on Exercise 58

For many people, written preparation for exercises 57 and 58 can be helpful. Allowing yourself the time to create a statement that is both meaningful and personal to you can help to enhance your self-confidence, as well as help you to carry out this exercise to the best effect.

Although some people find it easy to voice a statement out loud, others prefer to speak the words in their mind. If this is the case for you, I would encourage you to build up gradually to speaking the words aloud. Time and time again, people report that saying and also hearing the words has more of an impact on them.

Tone of voice and rate of speech, as well as posture, are key. Play around with the exercise to increase its benefit to you. You may need to work up to a confidently delivered statement, first starting in a whisper and slowly building upon this. Rate of speech is important too, as you need to take time to feel what you are saying, allowing the limbic system to register it.

Finally, it can be helpful to engage in this exercise in front of those you trust and care about. If you are able to do this, make sure that you engage in some degree of eye contact, as visual feedback from others can be very important.

USING SELF-COMPASSION TO GUIDE YOUR DAY

It is hoped that as you've read this book you have tried all manner of compassionate exercises aimed at building your self-confidence. Hopefully, some of these will become part of your personal daily or weekly practice. What follows is a very brief yet powerful exercise. It is one that I personally use all the time.

I find that when I feel anxious about certain things at work, avoidance strikes. For example, I hate making phone calls that may be awkward, and so I will find all manner of excuses to avoid picking up the phone. When I eventually make the call, I feel an incredible sense of relief. I wonder why on earth I have been avoiding the task and swear that I won't do it again. Despite this, guess what happens the following week?

Well, without my self-compassionate practice, this pattern would repeat itself over and over again. I am not saying that I never avoid such things now, but on the days I practice this exercise, I tend to do what I need to do. I feel better about my work, happier with myself, and molehills don't end up becoming mountains.

Exercise 59: Guiding Your Day

Step 1: Take a soothing breath, calm your mind and your body.

Step 2: Bring to mind your ideal compassionate self or a compassionate role.

Step 3: Now, slowly and warmly, ask your ideal compassionate self or compassionate role the following question: "What can I do for myself today that will make tomorrow a better day?"

Step 4: Imagine how you will feel if you manage to do the thing or things you brought to mind in step 3.

Step 5: Take a soothing breath. Feel a sense of strength and warmth.

Step 6: Now be guided by your own compassionate advice.

USING SELF-COMPASSION IN DIFFICULT SITUATIONS

Many of the exercises in this book have been introduced with the explicit instruction that you should start with something easy, finding a place where you feel comfortable, and taking a certain amount of time for reflection. As time goes by, such practices hopefully will train your brain so that different frames of mind become more readily accessible and an integral part of your life.

But what can help you during difficult situations? I don't know about you, but when I find myself in a situation where my self-confidence is low or feeling dented, I tend to question myself a lot. I not only question what I have done but also what I might do now to make myself feel better. Sometimes, this results in my mind seemingly shutting down; at other times, it seems to blow a fuse. My anxious brain tells me one thing, my upset brain tells me something else, and my angry brain contradicts both, seemingly simultaneously.

This next exercise can help guide you in the moment. That is not to say that this practice guarantees that you will make the right decision or do the right thing all the time, but it can help. I find it invaluable.

Exercise 60: Using Self-Compassion in Difficult Situations

When you find yourself in the middle of a difficult situation:

Step 1: Take a soothing breath.

Step 2: Alter your posture and maybe your facial expression in a way that will evoke a sense of compassion and a sense of calmness and strength.

Step 3: Take a moment.

Step 4: Now let this frame of mind guide you.

Reflection on Exercise 60

This exercise is aimed at altering your frame of mind in difficult situations, with the aim of altering the way you feel, the thoughts that you have, what you attend to, and what action, or inaction, you take. You are consciously stepping out of your threat system and into a compassionate mindset.

When engaging in this practice, you may find that a simple change in position can help change your perspective. If standing, you can take a step to one side. If sitting, you can adjust your posture, maybe shifting your weight on the seat, crossing or uncrossing your legs, or simply adjusting yourself against the back of the chair. As you have hopefully experienced, small postural changes can have a significant impact.

Conjuring compassionate imagery or the ideal compassionate self is not the only way of quickly changing your frame of mind. Some people have described how imagining a particular color can help them, while others have found the use of a familiar scent on a tissue or handkerchief to be a quick and beneficial way for them to gain a clearer perspective on a situation and regain their self-confidence. You may have found some of these strategies helpful while practicing previous exercises in this book. If so, it may be useful to adopt them in conjunction with this exercise.

CONCLUSIONS

This chapter gave you a number of different strategies to help you build your self-confidence. The final chapter will take what you have found helpful so far and translate it into a regular form of practice to equip you for your onward journey.

14

Reflections and
Future Directions

Life can only be understood backwards; but it must be lived forwards.

—Soren Kierkegaard

The early chapters of this book discussed how self-confidence is something we build and maintain rather than something we either have or haven't got. It is hoped that this new understanding will help counteract some of the shame and self-criticism you may have experienced in relation to low self-confidence. In addition, thinking about self-confidence in this way will hopefully help you develop a sense that things can change.

This book presented the evolutionary origins of self-confidence, how and why we often undermine ourselves, and how developing self-compassion can help. Understanding ourselves can be a further key to letting go of our self-criticism and shame and directing us toward more fertile ground on which we can build our self-confidence. That is why this book also explored the way our biological makeup and life experiences can affect us, the ways we then learn to cope with life, and the unintended drawbacks and consequences we often encounter.

This book explored what compassion is and how the views we have of ourselves can stop us from developing it. That is, contrary to the popular view that self-compassion is the easy option, wishy-washy, or involves letting ourselves off the hook, the development of self-compassion can be a difficult path to tread, one that requires strength and courage. It involves our confronting our past, our present, and our future and all that they bring with them.

You prepared for the development or enhancement of compassion with a number of exercises. You learned about various ways of practicing mindfulness. You then went on to practice soothing-rhythm breathing and finding a place of contentment. You used compassionate imagery in a number of ways, ranging from exploring how compassion feels in the mind and body to embodying the ideal compassionate self to developing a compassionate coach, companion, teacher, or nurturer.

Finally, compassionate thinking, letter writing, and behaviors, as well as a number of other exercises were introduced as a means for you to address your self-criticism and feelings of shame and ultimately find ways to further build your self-confidence.

This chapter will now focus on two final areas:

- Looking at your life as a story of strength and resilience

- Developing a template for self-practice that will build your self-confidence further

It is hoped that these two things will help you develop a more balanced view of yourself and give you a plan for the future.

LOOKING AT YOUR LIFE AS A STORY OF STRENGTH AND RESILIENCE

This book often has reflected on the amazing capacities we human beings possess. It has shown the way in which a combination of influences and experiences leads us to adopt certain ways of thinking, feeling, and behaving. When circumstances lead us to struggle with our self-confidence, we can become more prone to avoid things, adopt a social mask with others, or constantly strive in vain for perfection, engage in self-criticism, and experience high levels of anxiety and shame.

Hopefully, the formulation exercise in chapter 4 allowed you to gain a greater understanding of how past experiences might have affected you and your coping methods. It's also quite likely that the formulation you developed failed to recognize your resilience, strength, and other positive attributes. The following exercise is therefore designed to redress the balance.

Exercise 61: Updating Your Formulation

Before you begin, have your formulation available (see diagram 4). Find a place that is, as far as possible, free from distractions, somewhere you can be for ten to fifteen minutes. Sit in a relaxed, open posture that has strength or alertness in it. It is a good idea to close your eyes for the start of this exercise, but you may prefer to lower your gaze instead and settle it on a low fixed point.

If it is helpful to you, start by using your soothing-rhythm breathing or place-of-contentment imagery. Alternatively, use one of the mindfulness practices from chapter 7. After some minutes, bring to mind your ideal compassionate self or compassionate coach, teacher, companion, or perfect nurturer. With the help of this image, evoke your compassionate mindset, reminding yourself of all the key qualities this brings with it.

When you are ready, review the "influences and experiences" box in your formulation. Take a few soothing breaths as you review the information held there. Now, with the warmth of your compassionate mind, slowly ask yourself the following questions, allowing yourself time to think and reflect on each one:

- *Given that I have coped with these things, what can I compassionately conclude about myself?*

- *How can I view my strengths and qualities?*

- *Although such influences and experiences have resulted in difficulties, are there any positives that have come out of them? For example, do my difficulties make me more sensitive to the needs of others?*

If you have been able to come up with some compassionate views or conclusions about yourself, add a new box to your formulation, labeling it "key strengths and qualities." Add this box underneath the "influences and experiences" box and draw an arrow from the old box to the new one (see Andy's updated formulation in diagram 6 as an oxample). Now write down your compassionate conclusions inside the new box.

Once you have done this, take a soothing breath and return to the questions again, allowing yourself time to draw further compassionate conclusions.

Return to your soothing-rhythm breathing, feeling a sense of things slowing down. Now, with warmth, slowly read over each of the key strengths and qualities you have written down. Consider each in turn. Allow them to sink in.

• *Andy's Story Continued*

As time passed, Andy began to recognize that the formulation he had worked on so diligently seemed to give only one side of his life story (see diagram 3). He therefore set about redressing this imbalance. Reviewing the notes and letters he had written in his journal and looking at the questions provided in exercise 61, he began drawing ideas together relating to his resilience, strength, and other positive attributes. Andy then used this information to update his formulation (see diagram 6).

Once the exercise was completed, Andy took a few soothing breaths and read it through. As he did so, he felt his self-confidence building further. Andy was so positive about the experience over the following months that he returned to his formulation again and again to update it with new insights.

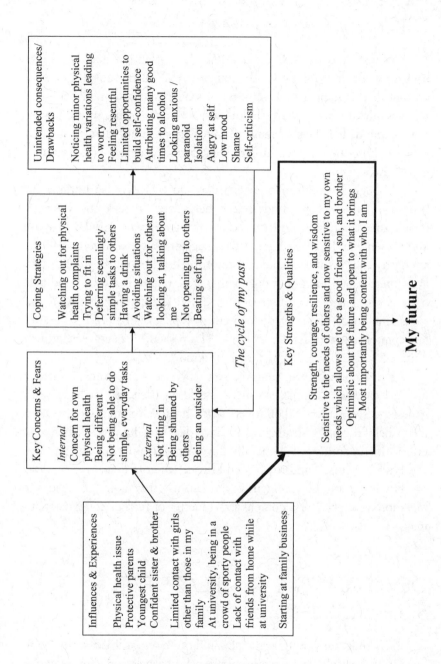

Diagram 6: Andy's updated formulation

Reflection on Exercise 61

You may find this exercise taxing. Your attention may be drawn back to difficult memories and thoughts. This is, of course, perfectly normal. If this happens, be mindful of where your attention has gone and warmly direct it back to the questions you are asking your compassionate mind. If it helps, break off and engage in an exercise such as your soothing-rhythm breathing or some form of imagery before returning to the exercise.

Although I would encourage you to do this exercise initially on your own, some people find that it helps later to seek the views of people they trust. How do they see you in light of your influences (past and present) and experiences? If they suggest that you have additional strengths and qualities, make a note of these. Then revisit the exercise and consider the additional points that were raised. Let your mind and body absorb these new observations. If you feel comfortable with the statements made about you, add them to your formulation. If you don't feel comfortable writing, for example, "I am kind," it may be helpful to write, "My friend Joe thinks that I am kind."

At this point in your journey, you may also want to make further updates to your formulation, such as adding positive influences and experiences you have had or are currently having. You may wish to note down helpful coping strategies you have discovered and their benefits. All of this updating will hopefully have a positive impact on the view you have of yourself and further build your self-confidence.

Finally, as you did previously, you can use this more balanced formulation as a focus for a compassionate letter or further compassionate imagery.

DEVELOPING A TEMPLATE FOR SELF-PRACTICE

It is likely that many of the principles and exercises outlined in this book have been helpful to you, while others have been less so. For example, you may have found the soothing-rhythm breathing exercise really helpful yet not achieved the same sense of calmness and warmth from engaging with place-of-contentment imagery. This is absolutely normal and is why the compassionate-mind approach introduces a range of different exercises in the hope that you will find some of benefit to you.

Throughout this book, your attention has been brought to your personal practice summary sheet, where you were asked to keep notes on the effectiveness of each exercise and to record any additional observations that you wished to make. Alternatively, you may have chosen to summarize your experience in your notebook or journal.

Have your personal practice summary available as you complete the final exercise, in which you will formulate a self-practice plan using the exercises that you know work best for you.

Exercise 62: Your Personal Plan for the Future

Use the following worksheet to record the exercises from this book that are most likely to help you continue to build your self-confidence and develop your compassionate mind.

Worksheet 13: Your Personal Practice Plan for the Future

Things that you have found helpful and would hope to practice daily:

_____

_____

What will help you keep up this practice? _____

_____

Things that you have found helpful and would hope to practice weekly:

_____

_____

What will help you keep up this practice? _____

_____

Things that you have found helpful and would hope to practice at certain intervals:

_____

_____

What will help you keep up this practice? _____

_____

Things that you have found helpful and would hope to practice when times are difficult:

_____

_____

What will help you keep up this practice? _____

_____

Things that you have found helpful and would hope to practice when things are going well:

_____

_____

What will help you keep up this practice? _____

_____

The following worksheet shows the personal practice plan that James created after reviewing his personal practice summary.

James's Worksheet: A Personal Practice Place for the Future

Things that you have found helpful and would hope to practice daily:

Mindfulness when I walk the dog; switching my focus from one sense to another.

Toward the end of the walk, I will evoke my ideal compassionate self, whose perspective I will take when I look ahead to the rest of the day.

Soothing-rhythm breathing just before I go into work.

Asking myself, "What can I do today that will make tomorrow a better day?" after my first hot drink of the day. I will use my compassionate-coach imagery to evoke a compassionate mindset before I do this.

What will help you keep up this practice?

Having the prompts of the walk, the drink, and going into work will help. Write this plan up again on a card and keep it in my journal.

Review on the first of the month how I have done.

Things that you have found helpful and would hope to practice weekly:

On a Sunday, I will write a compassionate letter to myself, using imagery first.

On a Saturday morning, I will practice my imagery, allowing myself thirty minutes.

In this exercise, I will ask my compassionate coach to help me design a compassionate behavioral experiment, aimed at building my self-confidence, for the week ahead.

What will help you keep up this practice?

I will write it on my calendar until the end of the year.

I will try not to book other things in at those times, and if I do, I will move the practice elsewhere and make a note of it.

Things that you have found helpful and would hope to practice at certain intervals:

> *I will schedule going every couple of months for a walk somewhere beautiful and to practice mindful walking. When I stop for breaks, I will evoke my compassionate coach and use this perspective to reflect on the time since I last did a weekend walk and look ahead to the weeks before my next one.*

> *At the end of each month, I will use chair work to help me see my present situation from both my day-to-day perspective and then from my compassionate coach's perspective. I will set aside evenings on my calendar for this.*

What will help you keep up this practice?

> *Entries on the calendar.*

> *Monthly review points.*

Things that you have found helpful and would hope to practice when times are difficult:

> *All of the above plus the following:*

> *Compassionate alternative-thought worksheets on the days things are difficult. Review the "taking action" chapter.*

> *Sitting in the presence of my compassionate coach with the difficulties I am having.*

> *If I am having difficulties with someone else, looking at their situation from my ideal compassionate self's perspective; doing this in the evening following any difficulty.*

> *In difficult situations, taking a soothing breath, adjusting my posture, and imagining warmth with (if appropriate) a slight smile on my face.*

> *Compassionate letter writing.*

> *Maybe doing slightly different things each day to help gain a broader and richer compassionate perspective.*

What will help you keep up this practice?

Knowing it works.

Reading my letters to myself to reinforce this.

Things that you have found helpful and would hope to practice when things are going well:

Savor the experience.

If someone has said something positive or acted toward me positively, making a note of it on my formulation.

Updating my formulation at set intervals.

What will help you keep up this practice?

Slowing down and noticing positive experiences. Keeping my journal with me as a reminder.

Doing all of the above will help me further tune my mind to increased self-confidence.

Reflection on Exercise 62

Remember that this is a compassionate plan to help build both your self-confidence and your compassionate mind. You can adjust and amend it, in light of new experiences, at any time.

Also remember that you are planning here for what you hope to do. Life gets in the way for all of us sometimes. We can get caught up in all manner of things that divert us from our original aim. This is often most true in the early days, years, and months of self-practice. When you do notice that you have wandered away from your plan, refamiliarize yourself with the work you have done to date. Then reflect on why you may have veered away from your plan, as this may give you some insight into the obstacles that have been raised and help you focus your mind on how to negotiate them. Finally, rethink your plan. If necessary, adjust it and then resume your journey.

FINAL THOUGHTS

As mentioned at the start of this book, in years gone by I would have been unable to hand over the final draft of this book without experiencing crippling self-criticism. As a young adult, I was convinced that if people truly knew me they wouldn't like me or, at best, would be indifferent. My mind was plagued by self-doubt, regrets, worries, and at times I was emotionally all over the place.

It's not that I think I am brilliant now: it's something better than that. I can warmly accept myself, warts and all. I can be compassionate toward myself and also feel more connected with others. This sense that we are all in it together is very different from the treadmill of constantly comparing myself favorably or, more commonly, unfavorably to other people. This has made me more self-confident and ultimately more content.

I wouldn't claim that all of this has been a result of the application of the compassionate-mind approach to my life. I had traveled some way down the path to self-confidence and self-compassion already, but this approach certainly accelerated the process. My continued practice helps me maintain a healthy state of mind by being more resilient to life's setbacks.

It takes time to forge a new path. We have to overcome obstacles, negotiate a tendency to walk the more familiar route, be courageous. Having said that, I think—and, most importantly, know from my own experience—that the rewards are worth it.

I sincerely wish you all the best in the next stage of your journey.

Resources

FURTHER READING

You will find listed below a number of publications on different topics that may be of interest to you. Some of them are referred to within this book, while others I would recommend as further reading should you wish to explore a particular topic in depth.

Acceptance and commitment therapy (ACT): Steven Hayes and Spencer Smith, *Get Out of Your Mind and Into Your Life* (New Harbinger, 2005)

Anger: Russell Kolts, *The Compassionate-Mind Guide to Managing Your Anger* (New Harbinger, 2012).

Anxiety and social confidence: Lynne Henderson, *The Compassionate-Mind Guide to Building Social Confidence: Using Compassion-Focused Therapy to Overcome Shyness and Social Anxiety* (New Harbinger, 2012); Susan Jeffers, *Feel the Fear and Do It Anyway* (Random House, 1987).

Attachment and brain development: Louis Cozolino, *The Neuroscience of Human Relationships: Attachment and the Developing Brain* (Norton, 2007).

Compassion: Christopher K. Germer, *The Mindful Path to Self-Compassion* (Guilford Press, 2009); Paul Gilbert, *Compassion: Conceptualisations, Research and Use in Psychotherapy* (Routledge, 2005) and *The Compassionate Mind: A New Approach to Life's Challenges* (New Harbinger, 2010).

Depression: Paul Gilbert, *Overcoming Depression: A Self-Help Guide to Using Cognitive Behavioural Techniques* (Robinson, 2009, 3rd edition).

Difficulties associated with eating: Susan Albers, *Eating Mindfully: How to End Mindless Eating and Enjoy a Balanced Relationship with Food* (New Harbinger, 2003); Kenneth Goss, *The Compassionate-Mind Guide to Ending Overeating* (New Harbinger, 2011).

General self-help: Elizabeth Lesser, *Broken Open: How Difficult Times Can Help Us Grow* (Villard Books, 2004).

Science of the brain: John Arden and Lloyd Linford, *Brain-Based Therapy with Adults* (Wiley, 2009); John Arden, *Rewire Your Brain* (Wiley, 2010); Susan Begley, *The Plastic Mind* (Constable, 2009).

Self-Compassion: Kristin Neff, *Self-Compassion: Stop Beating Yourself Up and Leave Insecurity Behind* (HarperCollins, 2011).

Shame: Paul Gilbert and Bernice Andrews, *Shame: Interpersonal Behaviour, Psychopathology, and Culture* (Oxford University Press, 1998); Jasvinder Sanghera, *Shame* (Hodder and Stoughton, 2007).

Stress in response to compassion: Helen Rockliff, Paul Gilbert, Kirsten McEwan, Stafford Lightman, and David Glover, "An Exploration of Heart-Rate Variability and Salivary Cortisol Responses to Compassion-Focused Imagery," *Journal of Clinical Neuropsychiatry*, 5, 2008, 132–39.

Trauma: Deborah Lee with Sophie James, *The Compassionate Mind Approach to Recovering from Trauma* (Robinson, 2012).

ORGANIZATIONS AND WEBSITES

The following organizations and websites may be of help or interest to you:

British Association for Behavioural and Cognitive Psychotherapies (www.babcp.com)

Predominantly set up for therapists, the website includes a section for the public that contains information on cognitive behavior therapy, self-help, and how to find a private therapist.

Centre for Compassion and Altruism Research (http://ccare.stanford.edu/)

Set up by Professor James Doty for international work for the advancement of compassion.

Compassionate Mind Foundation (www.compassionatemind.co.uk)

In 2007, Paul Gilbert and a number of colleagues (including myself) set up a charity called the Compassionate Mind Foundation. On this website, you will find various learning resources and details of other sites that look at different aspects of compassion. You will also find a lot of material that you can use for meditation on compassion.

Living Life to the Full (www.livinglifetothefull.com)

Set up by Dr. Chris Williams and based on the principles of cognitive behavior therapy, this website provides access to practical and user-friendly training in life skills. Web-based sessions focus on such areas as mood, anxiety, sleep, and confidence.

Mind (www.mind.org.uk; tel. 0300 123 3393)

Mind is a charity aimed at promoting better mental health. It provides high-quality information and advice on a wide range of mental-health issues.

Mind and Life Institute (www.mindandlife.org)

The Dalai Lama has forged relationships with Western scientists to research and develop a more compassionate way of living. More information can be found on the website.

MoodGYM (www.moodgym.anu.edu.au)

Based on the principles of cognitive behavior therapy, MoodGYM was designed at the Centre for Mental Health Research of the Australian National University and is a free Web program designed to help prevent depression.

Self-Compassion (www.self-compassion.org)

Dr. Kristin Neff is one of the leading researchers into self-compassion.

References

INTRODUCTION

A seminal book on compassion, covering why and how to develop it for ourselves: P. Gilbert, *The Compassionate Mind: A New Approach to Life's Challenges* (New Harbinger, 2010).

CHAPTER 2

On the science behind the three types of emotion regulation systems: R. A. Depue and J. V. Morrone-Strupinsky, "A Neurobehavioural Model of Affiliative Bonding," *Behavioral and Brain Sciences*, 28 (3), 2005, 313–95.

On the threat system: R. F. Baumeister, E. Bratslavsky, C. Finkenauer, and K. D. Vohs, "Bad Is Stronger than Good," *Review of General Psychology*, 5 (4), 2001, 323–70.

On modern society and how it intentionally overstimulates the drive and acquisition system: J. M. Twenge, B. Gentile, C. N. DeWall,

D. S. Ma, K. Lacefield, and D. R. Schurtz, "Birth Cohort Increases in Psychopathology amongst Young Americans 1938–2007: A Cross Temporal Meta-Analysis of the MMPI," *Clinical Psychology Review*, 30 (2), 2010, 145–54.

On the importance of good attachment with our caregivers: S. Gerhardt, *Why Love Matters: How Affection Shapes a Baby's Brain* (Bruner-Routledge, 2004).

CHAPTER 3

On shame: P. Gilbert, "The Evolution of Shame as a Marker of Relationship Security," in J. L. Tracy, R. W. Robins, and J. P. Tangney (eds.), *The Self-Conscious Emotions: Theory and Research* (Guilford Press, 2007), 283–309.

On reflected shame: J. Sanghera, *Shame* (Hodder and Stoughton, 2007).

On self-criticism: P. Gilbert and C. Irons, "Focused Therapies and Compassionate Mind Training for Shame and Self-Attacking," in P. Gilbert (ed.), *Compassion: Conceptualisations, Research and Use in Psychotherapy* (Routledge, 2005), 263–325; P. Gilbert, M. W. Baldwin, C. Irons, J. R. Baccus, and M. Palmer, "Self-Criticism and Self-Warmth: An Imagery Study Exploring Their Relation to Depression," *Journal of Cognitive Psychotherapy*, 20 (2), 2006, 183–200.

On motivations behind the goals we set: B. M. Dykman, "Integrating Cognitive and Motivational Factors in Depression: Initial Tests of a Goal-Orientation Approach," *Journal of Personality and Social Psychology*, 74 (1), 1998, 139–58.

On the different forms of perfectionism: D. M. Dunkley, K. R. Blankstein, D. C. Zuroff, S. Lecce, and D. Hui, "Self-Critical and Personal Standards: Factors of Perfectionism Located within the Five-Factor Model of Personality," *Personality and Individual Differences*, 40 (3), 2006, 409–20.

On the importance of self-compassion: K. D. Neff, *Self-Compassion: Stop Beating Yourself Up and Leave Insecurity Behind* (HarperCollins, 2011).

CHAPTER 5

Views of compassion: R. Davidson and A. Harrington (eds.), *Visions of Compassion: Western Scientists and Tibetan Buddhists Examine Human Nature* (Oxford University Press, 2002).

On social mentalities: P. Gilbert, *Psychotherapy and Counseling for Depression* (Sage, 2007, 3rd ed.); P. Gilbert, "Social Mentalities: Internal 'Social' Conflicts and the Role of Inner Warmth and Compassion in Cognitive Therapy," in P. Gilbert and K. G. Bailey (eds.), *Genes on the Couch: Explorations in Evolutionary Psychotherapy* (Brunner-Routledge, 2005), 118–50.

On distress tolerance: Susan Jeffers, *Feel the Fear and Do It Anyway* (Random House, 1987).

CHAPTER 7

On mindfulness: J. Kabat-Zinn, *Coming to Our Senses: Healing Ourselves and the World through Mindfulness* (Piatkus, 2005); J. Kabat-Zinn, *Mindfulness for Beginners* (Sounds True, 2006).

On mindful eating: Susan Albers, *Eating Mindfully: How to End Mindless Eating and Enjoy a Balanced Relationship with Food* (New Harbinger, 2003).

On mindfulness-in-schools project: F. A. Hupperta and D. M. Johnson, "A Controlled Trial of Mindfulness Training in Schools: The Importance of Practice for an Impact on Well-Being," *The Journal of Positive Psychology*, 5 (4), 2010, 264–74.

CHAPTER 9

On the importance of facial expressions: F. Strack, L. L. Martin, and S. Stepper, "Inhibiting and Facilitating Conditions of the Human Smile: A Nonobtrusive Test of the Facial Feedback Hypothesis," *Journal of Personality and Social Psychology*, 54 (5), 1988, 768–77.

On compassionate mind training: P. Gilbert and C. Irons, "Focused Therapies and Compassionate Mind Training for Shame and Self-Attacking," in P. Gilbert (ed.), *Compassion: Conceptualisations, Research and Use in Psychotherapy* (Routledge, 2005), 263–325.

On compassion-focused therapy: P. Gilbert, *Compassion Focused Therapy: Distinctive Features* (Routledge, 2010).

On "ideal compassionate companion" imagery: Ken Goss, *The Compassionate-Mind Guide to Ending Overeating* (New Harbinger, 2011).

On "perfect nurturer" imagery: D. A. Lee, "The Perfect Nurturer: A Model to Develop a Compassionate Mind within the Context of Cognitive Therapy," in P. Gilbert (ed.), *Compassion: Conceptualisations, Research and Use in Psychotherapy* (Routledge, 2005), 326–51.

CHAPTER 10

On our tendency to think in certain ways: C. Fine, *A Mind of Its Own: How Your Brain Distorts and Deceives* (Icon Books, 2007).

On how our old brain and new brain can conflict: N. F. Dixon, *Our Own Worst Enemy* (Routledge, 1987).

CHAPTER 11

On the use of writing as a means of promoting well-being: J. W. Pennebaker, *Writing to Heal: A Guided Journal for Recovering from Trauma and Emotional Upheaval* (New Harbinger, 2004).

CHAPTER 13

On assertiveness: D. Johnson, *Reaching Out: Interpersonal Effectiveness and Self-Actualization* (Allyn and Bacon, 2008, 10th ed.).

On random acts of kindness: S. Lyubomirsky, R. M. Sheldon, and D. Schkade, "Pursuing Happiness: The Architecture of Sustainable Change," *Review of General Psychology*, 9 (2), 2005, 113–31.

On acceptance: S. Hayes and S. Smith, *Get Out of Your Mind and Into Your Life* (New Harbinger, 2005); T. Brach, *Radical Acceptance: Embracing Your Life with the Heart of a Buddha* (Bantam, 2004).

Mary Welford, DClinPsy, is a consultant clinical psychologist who lives and works in the South West of England. She is a founding member of the Compassionate Mind Foundation, and she has been involved in the British Association for Behavioural and Cognitive Psychotherapies (BABCP) for several years. Working alongside Paul Gilbert, she helped to develop compassion-focused therapy (CFT).

Foreword writer **Paul Gilbert, PhD,** is a professor at the University of Derby in the United Kingdom. In addition, he is the director of the Mental Health Research Unit at Derbyshire Mental Health Trust, the founder of compassion-focused therapy (CFT), and the author of *The Compassionate Mind.*

MORE BOOKS *from*
NEW HARBINGER PUBLICATIONS

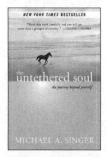

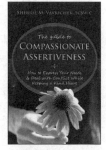